Spirit Quickening

Other books by Joanna Ormiston Long

The Cost (1996)

Come Life Eternal (1995)

Spirit Quickening

Thomas à Kempis

The Imitation of Christ

IN VERSE

Joanna Ormiston Long

PROVIDENCE HOUSE PUBLISHERS
Franklin, Tennessee

Printed in the United States of America

02 01 00 99 98 1 2 3 4 5

Library of Congress Catalog Card Number: 98-66186

ISBN: 1-57736-099-0

Cover design by Gary Bozeman

PROVIDENCE HOUSE PUBLISHERS
238 Seaboard Lane • Franklin, Tennessee 37067
800-321-5692

TO

THE HOLY SPIRIT

without whom I am nothing.

Contents

Acknowledgments

Without the help of God, SPIRIT QUICKENING would never have been completed. Sometimes I wanted to abandon the project but after prayer would return to it.

I am indebted to my family for their continual encouragement, love, and support. My eldest daughter, Ann Ellen Long, spent many hours reading early versions of the manuscript and offering valuable written comments. Her insight about words chosen by Thomas à Kempis so many centuries ago led me to many revisions as I attempted to express his ideas in today's language.

Writing about religious matters can be a hazardous occupation. Like a pesky weed, spiritual pride can creep into the most devout person's intent and smother the words of a sincere interpreter. Because I have always loved reading *The Imitatio* I wanted to share it. In this little garden of poems I have tried to give good riddance to weeds; and for any that remain I ask forgiveness. My dearest hope is that through restating Thomas's guide to spiritual development, SPIRIT QUICKENING can help others grow.

Introduction

The *Imitation of Christ* is a religious classic written by an Augustinian monk, Thomas Hammerken, who was born in the German town of Kempen six centuries ago. His manuscript became known throughout the Christian world and is still required reading in many Catholic schools. But students today are often discouraged from reading it because of its difficult archaic language. This version attempts to clarify its meaning, using simpler words that speak to all.

The source of the title, SPIRIT QUICKENING, is found in Book 3, section 34:

God's everlasting light surpasses all.
It sends down rays to clarify and gladden
the heart, to quicken the spirit with God's power!

A Note on Historical Background

The authorship of *The Imitation of Christ* has often been disputed. Some claimed it was written by more than one person and that Thomas Hammerken should be considered its editor rather than author. In the fifteenth century a controversy arose because some copies bore the name of Joannes Gerson, or Geersom, a well-known writer of that era, but scholars now agree that *The Imitation of Christ* was indeed written by Thomas Hammerken, from the town of Kempen near Dusseldorf, Germany. Thomas was born in 1380; his father was a farmer, his mother a school teacher. At nineteen he joined the order at Mount St. Agnes and became a priest in 1413. Much of his time was spent copying manuscripts. Among his original writings were biographies, sermons, and instructions for his fellow monks. He died in 1471, at the age of ninety-one.

Until the invention of the Gutenberg press, scrolls of *The Imitatio*, written in Latin, were circulated widely throughout Europe. When Richard Whitford's English translation was printed, it soon became the most popular devotional of the Christian world. In 1750 John Wesley said it should be read "a thousand times over." In 1833 Thomas Carlyle proclaimed it to be "universally read and loved by Christians of all tongues and sects." In 1860 George Eliot wrote that it "works miracles to this day." In 1953 both Norman Vincent Peale and Harry Emerson Fosdick called it one of the greatest of all spiritual writings, and Cardinal Spellman has proclaimed the work as "God's way to perfect peace."

The Imitation of Christ continues to be interpreted in many ways. SPIRIT QUICKENING attempts, through poetry, to make the message relevant to all who wish to lead a more spiritual life.

Spirit Quickening

Book One

On Living a More Spiritual Life

1

To follow Christ and to walk in his light
we study his words and think of his life.
To understand his lessons, we try
to live in imitation of Christ.
Mere knowledge of his word is not enough;
to love and serve the Lord brings wisdom and
better understanding. Too often we
think only of serving self. We seek ease
and comfort, pleasure, riches, honor, fame.
We love too much all things that perish.
We show little moderation. Yet nothing in
this world completely satisfies the soul.
To gain the grace of God, we must let go
of pride and vanity and place God first.

2 It's natural to want to know all things—
by nature we desire to know. But let
us place God first. We can love and serve
and try to know ourselves. If we know
just who we truly are, we'll turn away
from praise. No longer will we try to seem
so wise, for soul cannot be satisfied
with knowledge nor with words alone. A life
well lived brings comfort; an honest conscience leads
us to the Lord. The more we know, the more
responsible we must be. Let us not
be over-proud of any knowledge, art,
or skill; instead, let's use the gifts
we're given to help each other. Let us think
of all the things we do not know—
rather than of what we know. It's best
to be unknown; success and praise
bring pride in ourselves and envy within others.
Let's think less of ourselves and more of others.
We must not rejoice when someone fails,
or think that we are better—for we fail, too.
We all fail in various ways
and at various times. Yet how quick
we are to see the faults of others, while
our own we easily excuse.

3 We all seek truth. But truth cannot be found
within our minds or in our own opinions.
Not even in facts and figures may truth be found.
All truth proceeds from God; without that love
we cannot find the truth. If we want
to be attuned to truth, we'll establish

love within our hearts. We can pray:

> *Make me one with you in perfect love.*
> *Let all be silent in my soul*
> *that I may hear the inward-speaking truth.*
> *Grant to me the light of understanding.*

If we strive to do all things for God,
not for ourselves, we're set free to follow
the will of God rather than our own.
Let's keep our daily life in such good order
that we'll no more be bound to it.
Each day we'll try to overcome our faults,
growing ever stronger in spirit. We
shall love a life of order without becoming
obsessed with it. Let's love knowledge without
placing it above a life well-lived.
All things of this world must perish, and
learning soon fades as smoke in the air.
The wise will forsake their own wills to follow God.

4 May we consider well our words; let us
avoid impulsive actions. When we act
in haste, or easily accept the words
of someone else, we often err. Let
us beware of trusting our own judgment; instead,
we can seek counsel before we act. If
we live obedient to God, we will
be given help in making wise decisions.

5 It is good to read; the love of truth
will stir us often to read. But rather than

to choose a clever book, or one so praised,
let's choose to read the words that lead us more
toward truth. For of the making of many books
there is no end—and words empower us
to lie. The books may pass away;
God's truth endures. God speaks to us
through scripture, yet our pride may hinder us
from understanding. If we read God's word
with faith, and put aside our own desire
for cleverness or knowledge, we'll understand.

6 Our extreme desires create unrest.
They cause a restless spirit. When in our pride
we seek but self alone, we find no rest.
Unless we can subdue emotion and
our passions, we're led away from growth.
When we desire too much of worldly things,
and even when we try to ignore that desire,
we become unhappy. Yet if we
gained all of our desires, we still would find
no lasting peace. True peace of heart is found
through placing all our joys in God. Only
with the inward quietness that comes
from loving God and serving well
may we find our happiness.

7 Let us not put all our trust in others,
nor even in ourselves. Let's place our trust
in God. We serve the Lord by serving others,
doing all that's in us to please. Let's not
place our emphasis on wealth or friends,
nor on beauty, wit, or health—for all

things change. These gifts may sometimes be withdrawn.
While we have such gifts, we'll give thanks.
The purest prayer is one of gratitude.
God knows each one of us so well;
we'll be judged in God's own way,
a way that's different from ours. So let
us not become too proud of gifts, or deeds,
or any virtue we may have.
We'll think more highly of others than ourselves.
Peace rests light in simple hearts, but
a heart too proud, resentful, or filled with envy,
is heavy with unrest.

8 We can show goodwill and love to all,
but let us open our hearts to the meek, devout,
and simple, and to those who live well-ordered lives.
Let's open to them and speak out words of faith.
The desire to be with ungodly people, even
if they're famous, beautiful, or rich,
may lead us to become mere flatterers.
Insincerity can bring us close
to others, but it takes us far from God.

9 We can't always trust our own judgment.
Too much pride, and the love of freedom,
may lead us into disobedience
without just cause. Even when our reason
tells us to obey, we may rebel.
But liberty is found through discipline.
We need a discipline imposed when we
are young, in order to develop
the self-control that brings true liberty.

10 As much as possible, let's turn away
from anything, or anyone, who delays
our spiritual growth. This world can easily
enslave us, despite all good intent.
Sometimes when we're alone we find
the conscience troubled. We may have lied
or said half-truths. We may have tried
to offer comfort but became deceived.
True comfort is given inwardly. It
belongs to a higher power than ours. We
can pray for guidance; when it's right
to speak we can talk about that higher power
and encourage the spiritual life. Our own spirit
grows when we speak with those of like mind
and soul. Let us commune together.

11 We find inner peace, not through activity
in the world, but through study and
the contemplation of God. When we strive
to be truly simple and meek, we find peace.
Like the saints we can be free! Let
us give our hearts to God. Too often we
pursue our passions. To religion we
remain indifferent and cold. We
allow adversity to cast us down
and turn to others for comfort. But in
our need let's turn first to God,
the source of help. We'll be helped
if we trust God, and believe.
Each time we overcome a problem with
God's help, our faith grows stronger. In the end
the reward is great. It's for this purpose

our trials are given; as we overcome
we learn, more and more, to trust in God.
As we increase in years, our spiritual strength
should also increase. The only way to achieve
such growth is to trust in God—not in ourselves.
This is difficult; yet if we cannot
overcome the smallest problem of
each day, then how can we begin
to overcome the greater? At the start,
let's resist our inclination to wrong,
else little by little we may face
even greater temptations. Let us keep
in mind the goal of inner peace, give
our love to God, and strive for goodness.

12 Grief and adversity can serve a purpose.
They force us to see ourselves as exiles,
as strangers and sojourners in this world.
We cannot trust in worldly things. Despite
our good intentions we may be
misunderstood. Our misery also serves
to humble us, to remove our vanity
and pride so that we'll turn to God as judge
and witness. When we're troubled or tempted, or
when we're filled with wrong thoughts, we can see
that God is our necessity. Without
our Lord, we do no good. When we suffer,
we pray. We long to be free of this troubled life
and to be at one with God.

13 While we're in this world we can't be free
of temptation. Job compared our lives

to perpetual war, saying that temptation
is the enemy. We should arm
ourselves with prayer. But temptation also
serves its purpose, for resistance makes
us strong and wise, and able to understand
the temptations faced by others. Not one of us
is free from it, for it's within us as part
of human nature. But like the saints we'll grow
in spirit if we bear well our trials. We can't
escape from troubles. As one is overcome
another will appear. Even when
outward temptation is resisted, we
still battle inordinate desires of our hearts.
When we're troubled, we'd be wise to seek
good counsel. We can also be ready to give
counsel and comfort to others, with no
harsh criticism or judgment—for we are all
subject to temptation. When we place
too little trust in God, our thoughts may waver
and we become inconstant. Without the Lord
to guide us, we're like ships without a rudder,
tossed on stormy seas. But with patience
and the help of God we'll overcome.
Any temptation, squarely faced, can show
us what we are. But from the very beginning
let us resist temptation. As illness increases
when it's left untreated, so it is
with temptation. First, our minds admit
an unclean thought; imagination seizes
on it; and then the body is inclined
to follow it—and in the end we give

our full assent. Thus little by little we're
brought down by small temptations, unless
we wisely resist them at the very start.
Temptations vary with each one of us.
Some may experience more in youth, or at
the start of their spiritual growth, and some
may come near the end of life. Many endure
temptation throughout their lives while others
are only lightly tempted. God knows us best.
The state and merit of each one is known
and ordained, all for the best. Let's not
despair when we are tempted or troubled,
but pray for help in every need. We can
recall the words of Paul: that with temptation,
we're offered a way to escape. The choice is ours.
We're proven through temptation, trial, and trouble.
We are easily devout when we
are without adversity, but we prove ourselves
when trouble comes. And even while
we suffer, we can still hold fast our faith.

14 Let's try to look at ourselves objectively
and consider our deeds or thoughts instead
of judging others. We may judge wrongly.
If we truly try to know ourselves,
we shall grow in spirit. We need to have
a healthy love of self in order to
help any other person. But too often
we may love ourselves too much and try
to follow our own will instead of God's.
When all goes well, according to our own

desires, we seem to have much peace.
But if our lives go otherwise, we
become impatient or depressed. God
wants our love enough to help us rise
above our will. We can achieve this goal
through trust, faith, and love for our Lord,
who is always there for us.

15 Because we're judged according to intention,
rather than to how great our deeds, let
us do all things with love. Without the spirit
of love, what we do amounts to little
although others may praise us. Anything we do
with love is to our gain. It may not be
recognized nor praised; yet let us try
to do our best—all for the love of God.
Let's try to do as well as possible,
for others rather than ourselves. Sometimes
we're motivated by ambition or by
self-serving desires instead of love. But let
us be moved by love. A loving person
envies no one and aims to help another
toward greater spiritual growth. One who loves
will know that goodness comes from God,
that a single spark of loving charity
can be like holy fire to burn out wrong.

16 Let us be patient with our faults, as well
as with the failings of others. Faults are not
corrected easily; we must be patient
and endure our faults until God helps

us overcome them. Prayer helps us see
clearly and admit our faults. We
can pray about all human faults, asking
for patience to bear them. If we reprove someone
who won't accept it, we should not continue;
instead, commit it to a higher power.
Through grace and God's will, all things are turned to good.
We'll bear the faults of others patiently
for they have much to bear with us. And if
we can't correct ourselves, if we can't
be as we'd wish to be, how can we expect
perfection from another? We want others
to be perfect yet we will not correct ourselves.
We expect others to obey the laws that we,
ourselves, often disobey. We look
at others in ways unlike the way
that we regard ourselves. We should bear
each other's burden, for not one of us
can be faultless or sufficient, nor
be wise enough to stand alone. Let
us bear each other's burden and give comfort
in the name of love. Adversity
and troubled times show us what we are;
may our virtues and our love prevail.

17 Whether we're religious or not, controlling
our passion and desires will help us grow.
We must control ourselves in order to follow
the way of Christ. We may see ourselves
as pilgrims in this world. Others may see us
as fools, but let's be glad to be a fool

for the sake of God. Yet if we seek in religion
anything other than God and the health of the soul,
we'll find only sorrow. Let us always
find in religion a way to serve, not to
be served. Our beliefs will prove us, just
as gold is proven by fire. We can't remain
in grace for long unless we wish
with all our hearts to be humble, and to do
everything for the love of God.

18 When we compare our lives to lives of saints,
we see how little we do for religion today.
They served our Lord through hunger, thirst, heat
and cold, and poverty; they served through prayer
and meditation, and through their work.
They were persecuted. To follow Christ
they denied the worldly pleasures and suffered
torment and temptation. Yet still they prayed.
By night they prayed, by day they labored. And
their labors were fruitful, for all was for God.
They took joy in spiritual reflection
and in their work. They desired nothing
but God; they were poor in worldly goods
but rich in grace and virtue. Even when
they were in need, they were refreshed
inwardly by grace. They became
strangers to the world but dear, familiar
friends with God. Their lives glowed with the light
of virtue, meekness, obedience, patience,
charity, and love. Let us study
those lives as examples of devotion.

Our virtue is often measured more today
by what we do not do than by the deeds
we do. One who merely never offends
is often considered virtuous. Sometimes
we forget devotion to God, and through
our own dull laziness we forget
the examples set before us by the saints.

19 When we aim for good, our lives will shine.
Our inner and outer selves are in agreement.
Each day we can renew our hearts with love
and ask God's help to strengthen faith and purpose.
We can put the past behind us and
begin anew. Even when we fail,
we can succeed in keeping our goodwill,
and continue to try. Once we establish
the custom of morning meditation,
let us hold it fast; once broken, it
is hard to recover. Yet if a time of prayer
and contemplation must be set aside
to help a neighbor, it is soon recovered;
if lost through neglect it's hardly ever recovered,
and our spiritual growth is hindered. If
we cannot keep the customs of the saints,
we still can find one time a day for prayer
and meditation. At dawn we can renew
our purpose for that day; at night we can
review our deeds, our words, and thoughts. We need
to consider offenses to God, or to our neighbor.
In those private times we'll read or write,
meditate or pray according to our need.

Thus we become prepared to do God's work
on earth. And at any hour we're ready
to enter the kingdom of God.

20 Let us seek a time each day to spend
in meditation, to search the heart and think
of all our blessings. That time is only found
by withdrawing from the world, for
a while; from all things unhelpful to the growth
of spirit—from crowds and idle talk or noise,
intemperate people, or the running about in search
of thrills and pleasure. In other times, some have
renounced the world to serve a higher power.
Their lives remind us of the spiritual light
we too might gain, even with less
renunciation. We can be in the world,
as Paul maintained, yet not be of it.
That precious light the saints have sought
may often fade with excess talk.
Too often we exceed in words. It's best
to be alone at times, seeking wisdom
in our solitude. Then when we're
required to be with others, we speak more surely.
No one can lead unless he'd first be subject;
no one commands well unless he first learns how
to obey. No one speaks aloud
with surety unless he'd rather be silent.
Great leadership must rest upon humility,
the love of God, and all of God's creation.
If leaders hold true to ideals of service,
they won't give in to pride. The certainty

of bad leadership rests on pride,
on power, and presumption. But in the end
bad leaders deceive themselves and fall.
Whether we're religious or not, in
this life we'll never feel sure of ourselves.
Sometimes we're tempted simply because we think
we're immune to temptation; thus we fall
into spiritual pride. We think sometimes
we might do better if we could only withdraw
from the world; we think we'd know peace
if we could keep our minds on spiritual things.
But only at times may we ignore the world.
Our purpose here is to learn to love,
and to serve more perfectly. In our times
of prayer, in the secret chamber of the heart,
we can recall the advice of David—to stand
in awe, to commune with God, and to be still.
For it's in quietness that understanding
may be found. Through silent prayer our souls
are cleansed with tears of love and sweet devotion.
We're often moved by appetite and by
our curiosity. We go out
into the world only to return
with a troubled heart. A merry evening
may be followed by a heavy morn,
for pleasures can deceive us. Although they may
bring joy at the beginning, they often end
in remorse. What can be found that endures?
Nothing under the sun or moon. If we
were able to see all and know all pleasures,
would it not be in the end in vain? Let's

remember God and the commandments.
Let's subdue the foolish imaginings
and lift our minds and hearts to God—then
we'll find an inward peace. Yet we, being human,
delight in all things new, and so we must
sometimes expect to have a troubled heart
and a restless mind. It is our nature.

21 Joy is found in loving God and all
of God's creation. This includes ourselves.
A wholesome self-discipline will benefit
our spiritual growth. We'll examine the conscience
daily and truly repent our wrongs. Then
through prayer and forgiveness we shall find
peace and calm. We often take our wrongs
too lightly, and laugh when we should mourn. But
repentance brings us back to God, and we
grow stronger to resist further wrong.
Even when we're burdened by bad habits,
with God's help we can replace them with
the good. We should never use
as an excuse the actions of others.
Let's try to be objective, to see ourselves
clearly and consider our own thoughts.
It's wise to stay out of the lives of others and look
more to ourselves. It's better for the soul
to not be praised too much, yet all of us
love flattery. We seek it out. May
we think more of our souls than of the world
with all its vanities, and continue to pray
for the growth of our spiritual lives.

22 To live in this world is hard. We eat and drink,
sleep and wake, labor and rest—again
and again. Serving the body's necessities
is a burden. The devout would rather be free
of such bondage in order to serve God better.
We can't have everything according to
our will; not even the rich and powerful
nor the beautiful can have it all.
No one lives without some troubles. Worldly
goods become a burden, for only with effort
may we secure our possessions. Many of us
love too much our material things. But as
the hour of death comes near, we think more
about the soul. Why defer the time
to think about our Lord? Let's arise
and at this moment start! Now is the time
to love and serve, to make amends,
to put behind us negative things. Let
us master ourselves now and regain control.
We recognize how prone we are to wrong;
one day we do quite well, the next we fall.
One day our purpose is strong, our work is good;
but on the next it's as though we'd never stated
our purpose and intent. So let us be humble,
and never think that we are good. For we
are frail and only God is good.

23 A proverb says: "Today a man, tomorrow none."
We provide best for the hour of our death
by keeping our present lives in order,
by weighing each deed and thought as though

in the next moment we might die.
Tomorrow is uncertain; if we're not ready
for death on this very day, then how can we
be ready tomorrow? The fear of death is lessened
by keeping the conscience clear. Long life does not
always mean that we have gained. It is
a fearful thing to die—but it's more dangerous
to the soul to live many years. A long life
only increases our chances of doing wrong.
Every life must end the same. We'll keep
the hour of death in mind, each day directing
the intent toward that end. At dawn
we doubt we'll live till night; at night
we're unsure of living until tomorrow.
May we live each day in such a way
that death will find us always ready.
How happy and wise are those who live
in such a state! If we live our lives
with love, we can hope for a noble death.
Now, while we are strong and able, we
can do good deeds. Now is the time to consider
the health of the soul. Now is the time to gain
riches immortal by lifting our hearts to God.

24 In all things we behold the end. Before
we die may we subdue our willful pride,
resist all wrongs, think less of body than
of soul. If we love God we may be seen
as foolish in this world; in heaven we'll
find joy in Christ. In this world all things
are temporal. Love will give
us passage to a better world.

25 May we diligently serve the Lord.
May we love, trust God, and do our best.
Let's overcome within ourselves the faults
we most dislike to see in others. We'll follow
good examples, thus avoiding the wrong.
When we hear of all good works of others
we can try to do as they have done.
Let's think about our purpose here and keep
in the eye of the soul the life of Christ,
his passion, and his words. We can conform
our lives to his. We shall love and serve
with heart and mind, body and soul.

Book Two

On Developing the Inner Being

1 When we place our spirituality first,
the kingdom of God dwells in us. When we give
ourselves to God, we grow. When love is in
our hearts we know that God is in us, and
we're ready to receive gifts of the spirit.
We listen to our intuition; we
become aware of God's presence in our lives.
Let us prepare our hearts for that in-dwelling.
We know that if we love the Lord we'll live
according to his word. Through prayer we can
avoid all things delaying our spiritual growth.
Once we've found this treasure, we are rich!
God provides, defends, and helps us
on our way. We need not trust in any

other thing. The world must change,
people change; all things change
and fall away, but God abides.
We cannot always trust in humankind,
for all of us are frail. Those who may
be for us one day, on the next may be against us.
We turn as often as the wind.
But if we put full trust in God
and place that love above all others,
we'll be satisfied. Earth is not
our resting place. We are strangers here,
like pilgrims in the land, and perfect rest
cannot be found until we are united
with our Lord. So why should we seek rest?
All earthly things soon pass away.
If we cling to them, or depend on them
too much, we forget the spiritual life.
Let's direct our thoughts to God,
who gives us comfort in our troubles.
Jesus was disregarded in this world,
forsaken by his friends, and suffered wrongs.
We wish for no one to do us wrong.
Our Lord had enemies, and yet
we wish for everyone to be our friend.
How can patience be proven unless we endure
adversity? If we're unwilling to suffer
through our troubles, then how can we become
like Christ? We can suffer for his sake.
Trouble decreases our love for this world.
Once we overcome inordinate loves,
we turn to God. Our spirits are uplifted.

We find our rest in spiritual things.
As we are taught life's lessons, we grow wise.
We see things as they are, rather than
as they may appear to be. When
our hearts and minds are lifted up, we find
more time for prayer, for study, and good deeds.
When mind and heart are fixed in God, the world
can't harm the spirit. Let's apply ourselves
to daily life just as it comes along,
yet continue to refer all things to God.
Let's maintain well-ordered lives, thus
seldom arousing unkindness or pride. If
we love a worldly thing more than it should
be loved, we'll find it difficult to hold
our love for God. Excessive love of any
thing brings only sorrow. We shall place
those out-of-balance, inordinate loves below
the love of God—and know great joy.

2 Let us not be too concerned about
who is for or who's against us. Our
first thought should always be that God is for us.
If, in all we do, our conscience is clear,
God will protect us. Whom God defends
no worldly wrong can harm. Sometimes we suffer
through our troubles, but we must be patient.
When we pray God meets our needs. God knows
the time and place for our deliverance;
it's God's decision when and how to free us.
Any trial will strengthen the soul by leading
us away from pride. When we're reproved,

we then grow humble and try to improve.
Such meekness is defended. The meek receive
God's grace; they find much peace because they've learned
to trust in God, not in the world. And yet
unless we feel that we're less meek than others,
we cannot reach the spiritual growth we seek.

3 If we hope to give peace to others, we
must first find peace within ourselves.
A peaceful person benefits the self
and others, but one with emotions easily aroused
can turn the sweet to sour. Our passions lead
us to believe the worst. A peaceful person
is not suspicious of nor hostile to
another—but tries to find the best in all.
Those who aren't content within are troubled;
they cannot be quiet nor can they permit
another to be quiet. They speak when silence
would be best; they're still when words may need
to be spoken. They're much concerned with others but
neglect their own soul growth. Let's turn attention
first to our own souls. Let's regard
our neighbor in the spirit of loving charity.
How often we excuse our faults yet won't
accept the excuse of another. We'd benefit
much more by accusing ourselves, and excusing others.
The faults in us that we expect others to
put up with, we must bear in them.
We are far from perfect charity
and love. It's no great thing to deal with those
who please. It's easy to love someone who thinks

as we do. But to live in peace with those
opposed to us deserves much praise and
can't be done without spiritual help.
Our personal peace in this world will come
through patiently enduring our own troubles.
No one lives without some troubles, but
we overcome them when we turn to God.

4 Two wings can lift us up from earthly things:
One is intent and the other is love.
An intent directed to God contains the truth.
Pure is the love of God. When we can free
ourselves from inordinate loves, our love of God
grows pure. May we intend to seek the growth
of our own souls. That intent will bring
us liberty and peace and benefit
all others. If our hearts are right, we'll see
all creatures as a mirror of life and a book
of sacred law. There is no one so small
but holds some goodness. If within our souls
we know our conscience is clear, we can give
ourselves and all to God. Good conscience brings joy,
but trouble comes from a conscience that is bad.
Let's ask forgiveness and know that we're forgiven.
As iron is placed in the fire to be cleansed of rust,
so we become when we turn to God.
We are renewed. But if we lack the zeal
for spiritual growth, we turn to other things
for comfort. We may feel afraid to take
the spiritual path, but let us overcome
our fears. Let us try to walk the way
our Lord has shown to us.

5 We cannot trust too much in ourselves,
in our own wit and knowledge. Because of pride
and vanity we find but little grace.
We have less understanding, and what little
we may have, through negligence we lose.
We cannot see how blind we are. Often
we act wrongly, and defending the wrong,
we do much worse. We may be moved
by passion or zeal and think it is
our zeal for God. We look for neighbors' faults
but refuse to see our own. We complain
about the faults of others yet we don't
consider what they may suffer from ours.
When time is spent improving ourselves, we'll have
no time to judge another. Let's look to ourselves
and be silent about the faults of others.
If we wish to be attuned, to be
like Christ, we will not meddle in others' lives.
We'll take much better care of our own.
When we try to correct ourselves, we soon
discover how little the faults of others affect us.
Let's stop worrying about their deeds
and set our own before the eye of the soul.
Whatever we find amiss there, let us reform.
Let's place all other loves below God's love.
May nothing in our sight be greater than
the Lord, who fills all things with goodness and
remains the truest comfort of the soul.

6 Glory and joy are found in a good, clear conscience.
Let's keep our conscience healthy; it eases troubles
and sees us through adversity. But

a conscience clouded causes us unrest.
Wrongdoers may claim that no harm comes to them
because of their deeds; and yet unless they turn
to God, all they've done will come to nothing—
and all they've done will be undone.
When we love the Lord we turn our pain
and troubles over to the cross and know
we'll have forgiveness for our wrongs.
Worldly joys are brief and sorrow may
soon follow, but always we can rest in God's love.
Let us find happiness in good; let's live
a life of peace and goodness. In order to gain
an everlasting joy, we'll give but little
importance to this world. When we seek
out worldly things, we show how little we care
for all the joys of heaven. Let's disregard
both praise and dispraise; neither one makes us
better nor worse—for as we are, we are.
Whatever may be said of us,
we're no better or worse than as we're seen
by God, who searches our hearts and knows
us as we are. If we truly know
our inner selves, we won't care how
we're outwardly seen. The world looks on our faces,
but the Lord looks in our hearts. The world beholds
the deed, but God beholds the intent.
A good sign of a heart that's meek is when
one strives to do the best yet thinks that it
is little enough. Trust in God is shown
when one turns not to others for comfort, but
to God. When we lift up our hearts and

free ourselves of worldly loves, we reach a state of blessedness.

7 Let's love God above all others, even ourselves. The love of others can deceive us and often fail, but God's love will abide. If we cling too much to human love we'll find it fails—as humans fail. But to hold fast the love of God is to receive a blessed stability that lasts forever. When all others forsake us, God will not. It's often necessary to say good-bye to those we love, and in the end we must part whether we want to or not. Let's commit ourselves, living and dying, to the Lord, who is always with us— who helps us when we are forsaken by others. But God requires first place within our hearts. When we put other loves above the Lord or place our trust in any other thing, we may lose both. Would we trust a stick that can't support us, but lets us fall? We are all as fragile as the grass; our glory is like the flowers of the field, that in one day must wither and die. If we depend on outward appearances, we are deceived. If we seek comfort in anything other than God, we suffer a spiritual loss. Let us seek the Lord in everything. If we seek ourselves we may find self, but only to great loss of soul. And if we don't

seek God, we'll bring upon ourselves
more harm than all our enemies could cause.

8 When we do all for the love of God,
nothing seems difficult. Without that love
and God's help, everything seems hard.
Our efforts come to nothing and
we feel no inner satisfaction. In loving
and serving God, the soul finds inward comfort.
As Mary rose from her grief
when Martha reminded her of Christ's call,
so we discover happiness in
our own occupation, leaving our sorrow behind
and finding the joy of service.
Remember how it feels to be without
God's love? How dry and lazy we become!
How vain and foolish we are when we seek
material things. Those desires can harm
us more than if we'd lost the world.
What good is this world without God?
To be without that love is to live
with sadness and loss. But to be with God
gives us a taste of heaven. If God is with us,
no one can harm the soul. When we find God,
we've found our treasure. When we lose God,
we've lost much more than all the world.
Without the Lord we're poor;
finding God will make us rich. When
we're meek and peaceful, God is with us. If
we're quiet and devout, God can stay.
But we quickly lose God's grace when we

turn only to outward, worldly things. If we
neglect the soul, what friend then will we have?
Without a friend we can't endure.
So it's not wise to trust in other than
the Lord. Let's choose to have the world
against us rather than offend our God.
Of everything that's dear to us, may
we call the Lord most dear. We can love
all others for the sake of the Lord, and love
God only for God's sake. Christ is loved
for himself; he alone is faithful.
In Christ we'll love both enemy and friend.
We can pray for everyone to love
and honor God, and seek no praise and love
for ourselves. There's no one like God.
We can hope no single heart
is occupied with us alone, and that
we're not set upon one person. Instead,
may Christ dwell within us, and in all
good men and women. To truly know the spirit
of Christ, we must cleanse our souls
by putting aside the love of other things
and be united with God. When we are blessed
with grace we're strong. Without it, we are weak.
If we lack grace we mustn't give in to despair,
nor leave good deeds undone. Let's follow God's will,
turn all things over to the Lord, and wait
with patience. For after winter will come
the summer; after night comes day; and after
the storm we see once more
clear and pleasant weather.

9 When we possess spiritual comfort,
we easily turn aside from human comfort.
But could we be so strong in spirit that
we would bear the lack of both? How
can we endure a dry and desolate spirit
without seeking some joy for ourselves?
Is it a proof of virtue that we're happy
while we're in a state of grace? We all
desire to be in that state; we gladly
receive such consolation. To overcome
inordinate worldly loves, some choose God's will
instead of their own. We can follow
such examples. We can learn to do
without beloved friends—all ties of love
eventually dissolve. We can learn
to control emotions, subdue our passions, and
place all of our desires in God. When
we love ourselves too much, we follow other
desires and seek the comforts of the world.
But if we love God we won't depend upon
the world. The saints have given their all
for the love of God. They prayed the purest
kind of prayer—to offer thanks. We know
our blessings are given only through God's goodness,
and not of our own deserving. Let us not
be proud or presumptuous, but always thankful.
In times of grace, we must be diligent,
for that time of grace will pass and
temptation may then follow. When God's comfort
seems to be withdrawn, let us not
despair but patiently await renewal.
Such alteration of grace is neither new

nor strange, as many can attest. When David
was strong in spirit, he prayed to keep that strength.
Even when his spirits later fell,
he prayed against despair; he asked for God
to return him to grace and his prayer was answered.
Then David wrote a psalm of thanksgiving:
"You have turned my mourning into dancing.
You've put off my sackcloth and girded me with gladness!"
So it has been with the saints, and so it will be
with us. We mustn't despair when we don't feel fervent.
If sometimes we're cold, with an empty spirit, let's
continue to trust in God's grace and mercy.
Job also questioned those feelings of alteration.
He asked why God sends comfort in the morning
then each moment of the day withdraws it.
Let us trust in the grace and mercy of God,
for when we're left to ourselves and to our own
frailties, nothing can comfort us—
not the company of good people nor
the reading of books nor the hearing of hymns.
Nothing seems to help. At such times
our only remedy is patience and
the resigning of our will to God.
Not one of us can be so perfect that
we don't sometimes feel an absence of grace,
a diminished fervor and zeal. No one is free
of some temptation. But we know we'll find
the gift of contemplation only after
we endure our trials. The temptations
we resist may be a token of
the spiritual comfort that can follow.
If we stay stable throughout temptation, we'll

receive great consolation. God promised us
that we shall eat of the tree of life. Thus
is given comfort divine to make us strong,
to help us face adversities of life.
Temptations teach us to be humble, lest we
think that we deserve God's grace.
The enemies of spirituality
never sleep, and flesh is never subdued.
So we must always be prepared for battle.
We'll arm ourselves with faith, and trust in God
to help us resist anything that hinders
our spiritual growth and our good intent.

10 We are born to labor. Why should we
seek rest as long as we're on earth?
May we strive for patience rather than
for comfort, seek repentance rather than
delight. We'd all have spiritual comforts if
we could, for they exceed all other joys.
But we know our troubles will return,
for we are always quick to do our will
and trust too much in others or ourselves.
Grace is given to those who offer thanks,
but it's not easily seen by the vain and the proud.
It's better to be without consolation
than to let it take away our conscience;
it's better to do without our meditations
if they make us proud. The things we value
most aren't necessarily holy, nor
does our every desire make us pure.
All things sweet may not be good, nor
may all that's dear to us please God. If

we have known grace, as well as its absence,
we'll understand no goodness can come
from ourselves. So let us yield to God
that which is God's, and to ourselves
what is ours: In short, thank God for grace
and blame ourselves for whatever goes wrong.
With such a meek foundation, we may receive
some virtue. But virtue can't be ours for long
without that foundation of meekness. Those
who are great, in their own sight, are the least.
Those who are firm in their faith are not proud;
they ascribe all goodness to God
and seek no praise for themselves. They desire
only the joy and glory of God, and strive
always for God's honor. Let us be loving;
let's be thankful for even the smallest things,
then we'll be worthy to gain great blessings.
May we look upon the smallest gift
as great. If we consider the greatness of
the Giver, no gift will seem to be small.
Can we believe that pain or sorrow could
be gifts? Their purpose may be to renew our faith!
May we always be thankful for God's grace,
be patient even when we don't feel it,
and continue to pray for its return.

11 Many claim to love the Lord, but few
will bear the cross. Many desire his comfort,
but few his suffering. Many would feast
with Christ, but few will join in fasting. All
of us want joy, but few will suffer. When
we have no troubles, we declare we love

the Lord; as long as we can count our blessings,
we offer praise. But when we experience
adversity we feel forsaken and
we fall into despair. Often we
may hold a grudging attitude. But
if we love the Lord purely for
himself and not for our own profit, then
we'll thank God as heartily in times
of sorrow, temptation, or trouble as we do
in times of joy and comfort. Even if
we never receive consolation, we
can love and praise the Lord. How the love
of Christ can purify the soul! If only
we could give up our selfishness. Where
are those who serve God freely, expecting no
reward? Where can be found the poor in spirit,
who have no inordinate love for self or others?
Can any of us become so spiritual?
If we should give ourselves for God, it
would seem little enough, for God is great.
We may have much knowledge yet still may not
be good. Even if we have great virtue
and devotion, we may still not have
the one thing that we need. What is that?
To give up selfish desires and put God first.
Can we see what others value greatly
is not so great? Let's see ourselves just as
we are—undeserving recipients
of God's great love. We can love ourselves
as God has made us, and always love God more.
No one is richer, none more free,

none more powerful than one who can
place the self and all the temporary,
fleeting things of this world below
the love of God.

12 Consider these hard words: *"If any choose
to come after me, let him deny himself,
take up his cross and follow me."*
But even harder would it be to hear:
"Depart from me!"
If we follow the first we need not fear
the second. Let us choose to follow the Lord.
In God resides our health, our life and strength,
our virtue, joy, and perfection. The way of the cross
shows us the way to the kingdom of heaven and
to everlasting life. If we follow it
we'll be ready to die, as Jesus died
for us. For the love of Christ we follow.
If we die with our Lord, we shall live
with him; if we share his suffering
and pain, we'll be with him in glory.
By dying to the world we find our souls.
Wherever we go, whatever we seek,
we'll never find a surer way to Christ
than in the way of the cross. But when
we follow our own will, suffering
is always with us. Sometimes we feel forsaken;
others disappoint us; we disappoint
ourselves. Sometimes God allows us to suffer
with little consolation so we can learn
to submit ourselves. Through tribulation

and trial, we're made meek and humble.
This cross is always there—it abides
within. Wherever we go we can't escape
our troubles and trials. We must be patient.
Through suffering we find an inward peace;
if we gladly bear the cross, it
will bear us. It will bring us to
the end which we desire, where suffering
will be no more. But if we bear it against
our will, it becomes a greater burden.
When we try to avoid one trouble, another
surely comes—and heavier than the first.
Can we believe we may escape the things
no mortal can escape? The saints were not
without this cross, and Jesus suffered death
to rise again, to gain his glory. How
can we seek any other way to heaven
than this plain way of the cross? The end
of Christ's life held pain and martyrdom,
yet we seek only pleasure and joy.
Suffering can bring great spiritual
gain; as flesh is subjugated, soul
is strengthened. It's beyond our power
to bear our pain, to forsake the will,
to shun honors, fame or fortune, and
suffer all our troubles. But through our trust
in God we can bear all things.
The world and the flesh are subject to God.
Armed with faith and marked with the cross,
we need not fear. Through patience we're prepared
to meet the sufferings of life. When
we suffer for the sake of God

and die to the world, we have peace.
Everyone commends patience, yet few
can suffer patiently. But the more we die
to ourselves, the more we can live for God.
If there were any surer way
for the soul to grow than through suffering,
Jesus would have shown it by his word
and his example; he took up his cross,
asking us to forsake our wills and follow.
Thus we must conclude that through
our suffering and trials we enter the kingdom.

Book Three

On Learning How God Speaks to Us

1 When we close our eyes to vanity
and shut our ears to the lies of the world
we can listen to God's inward teachings.
God speaks to the soul. Those who hear
the inner voice are blessed. God blesses all
who seek the good, who work to improve the spirit,
who gladly serve and listen to the heart.

2 *Lord, help us understand your word.*
Help us know your way. We turn from those
who may speak well yet cannot kindle the heart.
They speak the letter but you declare the sentence.
They may show the way but you inform the heart.
They water the seed but you increase the growth.

They say the words, but only you can give
us understanding. May everlasting
truth speak clear to us. Let us not
be fruitless, as one who may seem loving
but is not.
We miss a great opportunity when we hear
your word yet do not follow it;
when we know your word yet do not love it;
when we believe it yet do not fulfill it.
Forgive us, and continue to speak
the words of eternal life!

3 God tells us:

Listen to my words and follow them.
They are sweet, and wiser than the words
of wise men of the world. Humankind
can't always fully comprehend my words;
they're not meant to merely please the listener.
Hear my words in silence, with meekness, and
with love. Receive them in a quietness
of body and of soul. From the beginning
I have taught the prophets, and still I speak
to all who listen. But many will not hear.
They listen to the world rather than
to me, and follow their appetites instead.

The world may promise temporal pleasures that seem important to us. We serve the world with great affection, and yet the Lord has promised life eternal; still, our hearts remain too slow

and dull to believe. Who of us will serve
the Lord with the same desire we serve the world?
None, perhaps. Why? We travel far
to gain a little money but for life
everlasting we scarcely move.
We work and slave for money; for the promise of
a bit of profit we will toil and sweat
both day and night; but for eternal goodness
and God's glory we are slow to seek.
We should be ashamed to be so slow
to serve the Lord, and sad that we embrace
the works of death sooner than the works
of life, that we will take more joy in vain
and foolish things than we will take in truth.
We are deceived by what we trust in most.
But God does not deceive. The Lord still comforts
those who love. What God has promised,
God will perform. What God has said,
God will fulfill. Goodness is rewarded,
although the soul at times is strongly proven.
We're told to write these words upon the heart
and think about them often. In times of temptation
they shall be a necessity. And if
we don't quite understand the words we read,
we'll understand when our Lord comes to us.
God visits those who love him in two ways:
through temptations, or in consolation.
Each day we're offered two lessons: one when our vices
are disapproved, and another when we are led
toward virtue. Temptations give us the chance
to choose; let us choose the good. And Trouble

comes to everyone, bearing in
his hands two gifts. Which one will you choose?
In one extended hand, Trouble holds
patience, courage, self-control,
wisdom, sympathy, and faith.
Trouble's other hand unfolds weakness,
cowardice and fear, isolation, and despair.
One or the other we must accept.
Which shall we choose? Only we can tell.

A PRAYER FOR GRACE

O Lord Jesus, you are all my riches.
All that I am or have is because of you.
What am I, Lord, that I dare speak?
Without you I am nothing.
You alone are good and holy.
You order all things, give all things,
fill all things with your goodness.
Remember tender mercies;
fill my empty heart.
Without your grace and comfort
I cannot bear life's miseries.
Let not my soul be like dry earth
without the water of grace.
Teach me to fulfill your will,
to live worthily before you.
You are my wisdom.
You know me as I am.
You knew me before the world was made
and before I was brought into this life.

4 God says:

My followers seek me with simplicity.
Those who walk in truth are defended from
all peril and danger to the soul.
Truth delivers them from the lies of the world.
Truth sets them free.

Lord, all you say is true. I pray your truth
will teach me, keep me, and lead me to
a blessed end. May I always
walk with you, free in spirit.

Let me say what is most acceptable.
Feel sorrow for your wrongs and don't believe
that good deeds alone will make you virtuous.
Remember that humankind is frail. Do
not glorify yourself, for you are more
unstable than you think. Seek the good;
let nothing else seem greater or more worthy
of praise except that which is everlasting.
Value truth and dread nothing so much
as your own wrongs. Some may not choose my way.
Through their pride they forget their souls and often
fall into temptation. Too much pride
will separate us, so search your own soul often.
Consider all the good things you've left undone
which you might easily have done.
Many have me in the mouth but not
in the heart. Devotion is shown in many ways;
some show it in books, some in images,
some in good deeds, and some in prayer.

Their reason is illumined with the light
of understanding. They do not love the world
too much, but seek the spiritual life.
In them dwells the spirit of truth.

5 When God comes into our hearts
we feel joy, for God is the joy of the heart,
our hope and our refuge. We're still imperfect and much
in need of comfort and help. We ask God:

Visit me often, Lord. Instruct me
with your teachings, deliver me from all
wrong thoughts and heal my heart so I
can be able to love you, be willing to suffer for you,
and stable enough to persevere.

Love is a great, good thing. It makes
a heavy burden light, it balances
the pleasant and the unpleasant, it bears
a burden yet feels it not. Love makes
the bitter savory and sweet. The noble love
of Christ, imprinted on the soul, allows us
to do good things. It stirs us to desire
perfection. We grow, more and more,
in grace and goodness. Love will turn the mind
to God, so we are not too much engrossed
with the world. Loving the Lord
can free us from worldly desires, so
the soul shall not be darkened. There's nothing
sweeter than love—nothing higher nor stronger,
nothing larger, more joyous, or full. What
is better in heaven or on earth than love?

For love comes from God. One who loves
can fly high, run swift, be merry in God,
and free in soul. One who gives all for all
possesses all in all, and rests in one
high goodness—God, from whom all love and
goodness flows. Such a lover beholds not only the
gift but the Giver, who is more than all gifts. Such
a lover is fervent and feels no burden
or labor as too much for the sake of God,
desires no more than can be attained, and sees
no impossibility. All things done for God are possible.
Love, therefore, does many great things.
Love may faint, but does not weary, may be
imprisoned, yet remains free. Love sees cause
for fear but fears not. Like a flaming torch,
love leaps to God and, through grace, is delivered from
all perils and dangers to the soul.

A PRAYER

You are my Lord, my whole love and desire.
You are mine and I am yours.
How sweet to serve You, how joyous to praise you!
I melt into your love; I'm bound in love.
I go far beyond myself for you.
I sing to you the song of love.
I follow you by uplifted thought.
I'll never grow tired of praising you.
I love you more than myself, not for
myself but for you. And in your name
I can love all others.

Love is pure and meek, joyous and glad,
strong and patient, faithful and wise. When
we seek ourselves and our own will, we fall
from love. Love is circumspect, not light nor vain.
Love is sober and merry, chaste, and stable.
Love is obedient to God; it is devout
and thankful. Love trusts and hopes in God.

6 Perhaps our love is not yet strong nor wise.
Why? we ask, and God replies:

With a little discouragement,
you leave what you began in my service.
You still seek outward comfort. Try
to stand stable in troubles. Pay no attention
to deceiving lies of the world.

God pleases us in prosperity but
displeases us in adversity. Can we
consider our troubles a gift given with love?
Through sorrow we grow wise. Consider God
the giver of all gifts, bad or good.
The gift of grace that comforts us
in this life is but a taste of the life
to come. Let's not depend on worldly comforts,
which come and go, but continue to strive
against the wrong. To despise all wrongs
shows our love for God. Let not our minds
be troubled nor afraid. Let's keep our intent
and purpose always whole toward God. Let's not
believe that faith is an illusion or

that devotion indicates a weakness. Let us
be patient with those who so believe. Many
may stand in the way of our desire
to be more spiritual. They ridicule
good works and try to hinder one's devotion,
or divert one from remembering God.
But they can't keep us from examining
our souls, or from a steadfast purpose.
Yet our own thoughts can hinder us. At times
we may grow tired of prayer and study.
We can tell our enemies, within and without:

Go from me! You'll have no part of me.
My savior, Christ, will stand by me.
I'll die before I give in to wrong. God is
my light and salvation; whom shall I fear?
God is my strength; of whom shall I be afraid?
For God is my help and my redeemer always.

God may speak, to tell that soul to keep
on striving against wrong:

If, through human weaknesses, you
are overcome, arise and then grow stronger.
Trust in grace.
And yet beware of pride, presumption, and vanity.
By these things, many are blinded and fall
into error. Let their fall become
an example, to keep your meekness of spirit.

7 Sometimes it's best to hide our devotion and
not speak too much about it. When we possess

the grace of devotion, let us be worthy of it.
Can we recall what it's like to be unaware
of grace? When we feel low and lacking in
the gifts of the spirit, we must be patient.
Let's not forget to pray, to keep on doing
the best we can. Let's not forget our duties
nor neglect good deeds, or grow restless.
When spirits are low we become impatient, and
we must then remind ourselves that total
devotion is not within our human power,
but is given through the grace of God.
It's wise to understand ourselves and know
the measure of our gift, the limits of
our strength, rather than to be prideful.
Let us use the judgment of reason. If
we presume to do great things, we may lose
what grace we once had. We will trust in God.
When we lack experience in matters
spiritual, we can also err
unless we're counseled well. If we think
that we are wise, we seldom listen to anyone.
It's better to be good than to be clever.
In times of spiritual gladness, let
us not forget when we've felt desolate.
In times of trouble let us not despair,
but keep our faith and trust in God. If
we're meek and small in our own sight,
if we keep our souls in order and
maintain our self-control, we may not fall
into pride, presumption, or despair.
So when we feel most fervent, we can consider
how we'll do when that zeal is gone. Remember

that joy will come and go, according to
God's will. Such alterations can improve
soul's growth. If we stay grounded in meekness
and fulfilled in love, if we seek God with all
our hearts and regard ourselves not too highly,
in the end we'll receive our great reward.

8 Let us not think more of ourselves than
we ought. May our pride be drowned in
the vale of meekness. When we feel weakest,
we understand just what we are and what
we've been and from whence we came. We learn
that we are nothing without God. All
of us are weak and imperfect without God.
But when God beholds us, we're made strong.
We're filled with joy; we
marvel that we can be
lifted out of our instability
and into the joy of spiritual life.
God uplifts us. Without God, we fall
back to earth. God's love will help
in our necessities. God helps us daily
face the troubles and peril of this world.
Through worldly loves we can lose
sight of God, as well as ourselves.
Yet when we seek again,
we find God—and ourselves; therefore
let us diligently seek. The goodness
of God never ceases to benefit
not only us, but all others as well.

A PRAYER

Turn us, Lord, to you again
that we may be more loving and thankful,
more meek and devout. You are our health,
our virtue, and all the strength
of body and soul—none else but you.

9 Both great and small, rich and poor can draw
from God the water of life, as from
an ever-freshening well. Those who serve God
with all goodwill receive grace for grace.
But those who glorify the self
cannot find spiritual growth. Let's
ascribe the good to God, not to ourselves,
nor to others, but always to God.
Without the Lord we have nothing.
Let's be glad that by knowing this truth,
pride can be driven out of our hearts.
When the heart is filled with love
there is no room for restlessness or envy.
Then we're not ruled by private loves because
the love of God rules over all. Our souls
are enlarged. If we understand
this truth, that love is all, we'll find great joy.
We'll fully trust that only God is good.
We'll honor the Lord above all else,
and in all things we'll be blessed.

10

A meditation

How great You are!
To we who love and serve with all our hearts,
You give the sweetness of contemplation.
In this way You've shown your love to me.
For when I was not, You made me. And when
I drifted far from You, I was brought again
to love and service. You are my fountain of love.
When I might have perished, You showed mercy.
You sent more grace than I deserve. What can
I offer for such gifts? Not all of us
can forsake the world to serve the Lord.
Yet it's no great thing that I serve, when all of us
are bound to serve. I marvel that You love me!
All I have and all I am or do
is yours; and yet your goodness is so great
that You would rather serve me.
Heaven and earth, the planets and stars with all
their contents have You created; they are at
your bidding. Daily they do as You command.
You give us angels for help. Above all else,
You promise to serve us yourself. So what can I give
to You for such great goodness? Would that I
could serve You all the days of my life.
You are worth all praise, forever.
You are my Lord and I your poorest servant.
I'll never grow weary of praising You.
All I ask is that I may always pray. Amen.

Those who freely submit themselves to God,
who forsake the world and choose to live
a disciplined life for the sake of God,

receive much consolation and freedom of spirit.
By such service we are blessed. When
we're in a spiritual state, we may help others
as well as pleasing the Lord. Let's hope
to serve with this intent.

11

A DIALOGUE WITH GOD

My children need to learn many things
they have not yet learned well.

What are these things?

Don't love yourself too much, and follow God's will.
Human desires and emotions make you unstable.
But you always have a choice; you can choose
to follow My way or your own.
If God is chosen, you'll be content
no matter what happens. But if your own will
rules your heart, you may be hindered or stopped.
Beware of seeking your desires without
first praying for guidance. Otherwise you may
be disappointed, even though at first
you might be pleased. Don't be too quick to want
all that seems good, nor too quickly refuse the opposite.
Refrain and be patient. Ask for My help in all
of your decisions. Resist your appetites;
let them be subject to the spirit within.
Delight in simple things. Whatever happens
do not complain. Always give thanks.

12

Because of life's conflicting events, our patience
is always needed. We cannot live without

some troubles and sorrow, but we can order ourselves
for peace. Even in the midst of troubles,
we can trust that peace is possible.

13 We may have to suffer the pain of this world
for the peace of the world to come. Some may seem
to gain all things that they desire. But will
it endure? Joy can vanish like smoke in the air.
Too often, that which brought us pleasure, later
brings us trouble and pain. O how short,
how false and fleeting are many pleasures of
this world! Worldly people don't perceive it.
Like dumb beasts they run headlong toward
their own destruction, all for a bit of pleasure
in this corruptible life. When we turn
away from lust and greed we find delight
in God. Let us fix our love upon
the Lord. If we'd have abundant joy,
we'll put aside inordinate loves. The more
we withdraw from worldly pleasure, the sweeter we find
the consolation of our Creator.
To find such joy and consolation, we
must try to replace bad habits with ones that are good.
It can be done, through the strength of prayer.
Those who disobey the Lord lose grace;
those who seek the self and private things
can lose God's blessings. Let the flesh obey
the spirit. Our enemies are crushed if
the soul is strong. When the spirit weakens,
self becomes the enemy.
We must learn to master self and overcome

our pride. We can learn to be patient and meek,
to break our own will for the sake of God.
Let's subject ourselves to the best in our hearts.
We've all offended God at times, yet mercy
spares us. The soul is precious in God's sight.

14 Sometimes we ask, what will become of us,
we who are lower than the angels? If
God found fault in angels and spared them not,
if stars fell from the heavens, then what can we
who are only dust and ashes expect?
Some who seemed so virtuous have fallen.
We have no holiness nor good without
the Lord. No wisdom helps but God's, nor
can anything help us except God's power.
If God should forsake us, we would surely perish.
But with grace we are uplifted
and we live again.

How profoundly do I submit to God—
O substance I cannot comprehend,
O sea I cannot sail!
My substance is as nothing.
What is flesh in the sight of God?
Can mere clay
make or glorify itself ?

15 Christ tells us to make known our desires in requests:

Lord, if it's your will, let it be done as I ask.
If it's to your praise, may it be fulfilled in your name.

And if granted, let me use this opportunity
to honor you. But if it's hurtful to me
and would not profit my soul,
then take away this desire. Amen.

Not every desire is spiritual although it may seem good. We don't always know when motives are good or bad, even when we seem moved by our own good spirit. Sometimes we may deceive ourselves. With meekness and the love of God, we can ask whatever we want but still commit all things to God.

Lord, you know what I need.
My life is yours. Do with me as you know best
and as it pleases you to do.
I'm in your hands. Lead me.
May I be worthy of your love.
I'm thankful for your grace. May it be with me,
unto the end. I want only what is
acceptable to you. Your will is my will;
may it always follow yours.
Above all, may I rest in you. You are
my peace, the perfect rest of body and soul,
so in this peace and in this goodness
may I always rest. Amen.

16 We believe there's an abundance of good in heaven. Our worldly goods can never satisfy us, but we can keep and use them in this life, yet still

desire the eternal good. Full felicity
is found in God, who made everything from nothing.
We may taste some happiness for a while,
but worldly comfort is brief. Yet a follower
of God will always have a Comforter.

17 God knows what's best and provides for us better
than anything we can provide for ourselves.
God is with me in the darkness as well
as in the light, and I am thankful. In
times of comfort or in times of trouble,
we still love God. We must be as ready
to suffer as to celebrate, as ready
to be needy as we are to be rich.
We can take God's hand in joy as well
as in our sorrow and be thankful for
all things that come to us. With God's help
we'll keep distant from sin and dread not death.
If our names are in the book of life
we needn't grieve, no matter what trouble comes.

18 Christ descended from heaven for us. He came,
not of necessity but for love, that we
might believe and accept his gift of eternal life.
Through his death upon the cross, we
receive God's grace. Meditate upon
his life: he lacked worldly things and he
knew shame—for his compassion he received
unkindness and for his miracles, scorn.
His doctrines were rebuked, his teachings ignored.
Yet he was patient, fulfilling the will of God.

Let us bear patiently the burdens of
this world. Life is often tedious
and burdensome but grace and love will make
a life worthwhile. With Jesus as our example,
we learn to love. If he hadn't shown
the way, who would try to follow? How many
would be lost without his blessed example?
Even when we've heard his doctrines,
we remain slow and dull. What would
we be if there were no such light to lead us?
We'd only fix our minds on worldly things—
and that would keep us from knowing God.

19 Jesus asks us why we complain. We
should cease and complain no more. Let's consider
his suffering and his disciples; then
we'll see how little we suffer for God.
We have suffered little in comparison
of those who suffered for God in times before,
who were tempted so strongly and troubled so grievously
and, in so many ways, proved. Recall
how others have suffered for their faith. If
our sorrows don't seem small, we can develop
patience. Whether our trials are small or great,
we should bear them as patiently as we can.
The better we bear the wiser we are, and
the more we gain. Burdens will be lighter,
due to our own goodwill. There's nothing we
may suffer for God without gaining. We must prepare
for battle if we want a victory; without a battle
we cannot win the crown. If one refuses
to suffer, one refuses to be crowned.

Without labor no one comes to rest.
Without battle no victory is won.

Lord, make it possible to me,
by grace, what is impossible to me
by nature. You know that I don't want to suffer.
Help me know that to suffer in God's name
is good for the health of my soul. Amen.

Our minds cannot be free unless we stop
continually thinking of ourselves. We
can have a healthy love and acceptance of self;
to love others we must first love the self. But all
who love themselves too much become covetous
and vain. They glorify the self. They are
needlessly on the go, seeking worldly
things that cannot long endure. They
are prisoners, fettered and bound with chains.
They lack true liberty and are not free
in spirit. All that is not directed or made
by God must perish. Let us give up seeking
out worldly things and find rest. But this
is not the work of a day, nor is it like
the simple play of children. As we consider
the lives and works of others who lived well,
we should not be discouraged, but follow them.
Let us desire to follow Christ and his teachings,
knowing that first we must forsake the self,
love God, and stay on the spiritual path.
This wisdom is precious as gold tried in the fire;
the world has almost forgotten it. Many claim
that it is true, but in their lives they do

not follow what they say—yet it's a jewel;
let's obtain it and strive each day to keep it.

20 We confess we're often weak, slow
to do good deeds and think of others. We
intend to be strong and more aware, and yet
we still choose the easier path, for it's
harder to give to others than to ourselves.
Christ said whatever we do to others, we do
to him; let us remember that. But God
knows our weakness and has mercy on us.
We're sorry to miss the chances to do good.
We grow tired of our constant battle
with selfishness; it makes us weary of
our daily lives. We ask for understanding
and help to see our faults more clearly. God
will give us strength to lead our troubled lives,
for when one trouble leaves, another comes.
We wonder how to love a life so full
of pain—a life that sometimes seems to be
ruled by disease, disaster, and death. Yet all
of us love life. We're thankful for its beauty,
and all its love and goodness. Even when
the world deceives us, we never leave it lightly.
Some things make us love the world, and some
things make us despise it. Only a taste of joy
can overcome the mind unless we give
full credit to God, the source of all. If not,
worldly delight can drive away our true
desire for heaven. Many live only for
sensual pleasure because they've not yet tasted
the sweetness of God, nor known the inner joy

that comes with goodness and grace, virtue and love.
Those who live in holy discipline
have learned the promise of heaven even as
they see the deceptions and errors of this world.

21 May we place, above all things, the Lord.
We pray for special grace to keep our God
above all creatures, above all health and beauty,
above all glory and honor, riches and arts;
above all fame and praise, sweet consolation,
hope and promise, merit and desire,
gifts, rewards and joys. Also above
the angels, archangels and spirits, above all things
visible and invisible, and above all things
that are not of God. In the Lord we find
all goodness, perfect and full; the best, most high,
most sweet and fair, most loving, noble and glorious.
Whatever we receive other than
the Lord is little. Our hearts rest only in God,
who gives us wings of liberty so we
can fly and rest ourselves in the Lord.
We complain about the miseries
of life and bear them heavily. Each day
can bring events that take our minds off God
or rob us of our good desire to serve.

O hear our inward longings, Lord!
Our hearts cry out without a voice—Come,
bring me comfort, for without you there
can be no gladness or joy. My soul seems
empty, imprisoned until you give to me
true liberty. Let others seek

out what they will. I seek nothing but God,
my everlasting hope and health. I pray
for grace to reassure my soul that you
are near. Lord, I'm thankful for your mercy.
By your providence, all things are ruled.
May my body and soul, my heart and tongue
forever praise the Lord. Amen.

22 We ask God to open our hearts and lead
us along the spiritual path. May
we always be thankful for gifts from God.
Some people receive more gifts, and some get less, but
every gift is God's—and all are important.
To those who are given much, much is expected;
may we use our gifts—great or small—
to God's glory, and remember that
without the Lord the least gift can't be had.
Let those receiving more not glorify
themselves, as though such gifts are gained through one's
own merit. We must never exalt ourselves,
and never disdain nor despise another. Those
who receive less gifts should not be envious,
but lift their minds with thanks that gifts are given.
Those who are most acceptable to God
are those who least consider self. For all
gifts, we should be humble and be even more
thankful and devoted to the Lord.
All things come from God, who knows what's best
and why one may have less than another.

23 How can we find peace of soul? There are
four ways to follow every day:

Try to fulfill God's will, not your own.
Choose less worldly riches; share with others.
Practice humility, love, and forgiveness.
Pray that God's will be done in you.

To follow these ways brings inner peace. Sometimes we may still feel discontented but these ways will benefit soul's growth and health.

A PRAYER

Lord, I ask your help.
Vain thoughts and imagined fears trouble me.
Without your help, I can't fight them off.
Drive out the pride in my heart.
My hope and comfort lie in you.
I turn to you in every trouble; I trust
in you. I call to you and patiently
await for you to enlighten me. Your light
drives out my fear and darkness.
Help me keep my conscience clear;
grant me purity of heart.
Command the winds of pride to cease;
bid the sea of envy rest;
still the north winds of temptation.
Bring me to your peace and tranquillity.
Send me your light and truth to illuminate
the barren earth of my soul.
Give me the water of inward devotion to moisten
the dryness of my spirit so I may bring
forth good, sweet fruit. Raise up my burdened mind
to help me love all heavenly things.

The consolations of others cannot fully
satisfy my soul. I turn to you.
Hold me with the bond of love;
without you I am nothing. Amen.

24 Let us not become too curious
about other people's lives, nor to be
concerned with things that don't involve us. We
can say: "What is it to me? I'll follow God;
what's it to me whether one is good or bad
or whether one says this or that?
I need not answer for the actions of others,
only for my own. Why should I meddle?"
God knows everything. All our minds
and wills are open to God to see. We
can say: "I'll keep myself in peace and let
all others do as they will. God knows what's best."
If we admonish others about their souls,
we cause trouble. By judging, we can lose
our own reward. Let's prepare our souls
by opening our hearts to God, by holding
fast our faith through prayer, by being humble.
Then we shall find comfort in the Lord.

25 Jesus said to his disciples: "My peace
I give to you—not as the world may give,
but much more than it gives." Some say that they
desire peace but won't do what is required
for peace. God's peace is with the mild of heart.
Peace can be found through love and patience.

If we hear Christ's words and follow them,
we'll have a plenitude of peace. Again
we ask: "How can we find such peace?" The answer:
In all your works, watch what you do and say.
Set your whole intent to please the Lord;
seek nothing without God. Don't judge the deeds
of others, nor meddle in matters that don't pertain
to you. If you follow this advice,
you'll seldom feel troubled. But also understand
that to be without trouble is not found in this life,
but only in the life to come. When you
are free of grief, don't think you've found true peace,
for trouble comes again. When all is well
—especially when everything seems perfect—
don't think that you are great in the sight of God
or especially loved because of your devotion.
A virtuous person is not known by gifts;
they do not indicate perfection. Then
what does indicate our virtue, we may ask.
When we can offer our whole heart to God,
when we seek little for ourselves and give
our thanks to God for everything, then
we come closer to being as God wills.
We can weigh all things in the balance of
God's love. When we are strong in faith,
it's by God's grace, so we should never think
that we are righteous or holy. Let us walk
the path of peace and keep the certain hope
of meeting God, face to face in
the kingdom of heaven. There we'll find our rest,
our everlasting peace and joy.

26

A PRAYER

Lord, help me serve
without clinging too much to other loves.
I ask to be kept from worldly concerns, that I
may care for necessities, yet not be charmed
by pleasures of the world and the flesh.
Preserve me from all that hinders the growth of my soul
and let me not be broken by fear or sorrow.
Free me from my pride and vanity,
and from the common sorrows that come with age.
The body's needs often hinder the soul
and dilute my desire to worship you.
Let not flesh and blood overcome me,
nor this world's brief glory deceive me.
Give me the spiritual strength to resist.
Grant me patience in sorrow and help me endure.
A fervent spirit finds that food and drink
and bodily needs, while necessary,
are troublesome. Grant me the grace to use
all things with moderation. To give up all
is not required, for life must be preserved.
But seeking too much of anything will cause
the body to rebel against the spirit.
I pray that by your grace I may be taught
to become more temperate. Amen.

27

We are told to give all for all, and that
the love of self can hurt us more than any
other thing in this world. But we
must hold a healthy love of self

so we can love each other. If our love is pure
and kept in proper order with God first,
we'll find freedom from inordinate loves.
Let's crave nothing that keeps us from our growth.
Let's commit ourselves first to God.
When we follow the will of God, nothing
can harm the soul. But if we seek this or that,
going here and there for our own profit
or pleasure alone, we'll always be restless
and never free of mind—for in each place we'll find
something to dislike. Even when we attain some goals,
we find no peace of soul. This is true
not only of gold, silver, and worldly riches,
but also of the desire to be honored and praised.
These things vanish and, like smoke in the wind,
soon pass away. Place means nothing if
we lack devotion. One may change the place
but it won't help without the faith in God.
The problems one has fled from rise again,
perhaps more grievous than before. We can pray:

God, give me grace to be strong in soul and spirit,
to clearly see all transitory things
as they are. For nothing under the sun
is lasting, and all is vanity. O
how wise it is to understand this truth.
Grant me wisdom to seek and find you
and, above all things, to love you.
Help me withdraw from those who merely flatter,
and to be more patient with others.
May I not be moved by every blast
of words, and bring me to a blessed end. Amen.

28 Christ told us not to grieve when others say wrong things about us. If our spirit is in order, we won't care about such words. It's wise then to keep silent, turn our hearts to God, and not let others trouble us. Any inordinate love, or fear, will cause unquiet hearts and restless minds. Peace cannot be found in others. No matter what words—good or bad—might be said of us, we are what we are. True peace and glory will be found in loving, serving, and pleasing only God, rather than others.

29 In times of trial and tribulation, we call to the Lord. Necessity drives us to God. We can turn those times of necessity to our spiritual gain. We can say:

O Lord, I see trouble
on every side. Save me in this hour!
Perhaps I've come into this trouble so
that I'll be humbled; then I'll praise
you even more when it's over. Give
me patience, help me to be brave and trust
in you so I won't fear whatever happens.
May your will be done.
I know that you can take away
this trouble, as you've often done before.
And when it's over I shall honor you
and praise you everlastingly. Amen.

30 God sends us comfort in times of trouble.
When all is not well with us the Lord says,
"Come to me!" But we are slow to turn
ourselves to God and to accept that comfort.
Before we go to prayer we seek out other
ways; we try to solve the problem ourselves
or look to outward things, without the Lord,
to no avail. Why can't we see that God
helps those who ask for it? Without the Lord
we find no remedies. But if we place
our trust in God and ask for help, we are
restored to grace. Nothing is impossible
to God. Where is our faith? In God we must
stand strong, be steadfast, and believe in
the promises God gave. Our fears may trouble
us, but why dread things to come? Fear only
brings us sorrow upon sorrow. We
can bear with patience each day's trouble and dread
not the troubles to come. We are foolish
when we worry about things that may never happen.
Let's put our trust in God. Even when
we feel that all is lost, God is near.
When adversity comes into our lives
we're never forsaken if we trust in God,
who knows our hidden thoughts; for soul's sake we
may need to endure some troubles so that
we don't become too proud or think that we
are better than we are. Our gifts all come
from God; can we perceive a trial as
a gift? If troubles come, let us take
them bravely, without losing faith. Soon

we'll be again uplifted and sorrow turned
to joy. Then we'll praise God even more.
If we can understand this lesson, hard
as it may be, we won't give in to troubles.

31 As long as transitory things rule over
us, we can't come freely to the Lord.
We need God's help to be wise and understanding.
O for the wings of a dove, that we might fly
to our Savior and rest in him! No one can be
more at peace than one who keeps the mind
and intent toward God. How can we hold
God foremost in our minds? Unless we free
ourselves of too many worldly desires, we can't.
Few will be quiet and contemplative, and few
people count the love of things less than
the love of God. Contemplation requires
a discipline and self-control, as well
as sincere desire to grow in spirit. A moment
of devotion lifts the soul. It unites us to God.
There's a difference between the wisdom of one
who becomes enlightened by grace and the clever one
who is merely studious. Any learning
that comes through God's power is nobler than
that gained only through study. Many desire
the gift of spiritual growth, but few will follow
its requirements. Since sensuality
can interfere with meditation, we
can practice self-control and make the body
subject to the soul. For spiritual growth
we first examine the inner self. Each day

we'll search the conscience and determine where
our true affections rest. We'll feel
great sorrow for the wrong deeds that we've done,
and yet we'll know we are forgiven. When
the inner self becomes corrupted, deeds
are necessarily corrupt. We want
to have a clean heart and bring forth good fruit in
our lives. We may question the deed someone has done,
rather than with what intent. Nature
will behold the outward deed, but God
considers the intent. The first
is often deceiving; the second is not.

32 Can we stop thinking of ourselves so much?
When we glorify the self, we
become vain, imprisoned by self love and
our desire for material things that cannot
long endure. Like prisoners, we
are bound with chains that fetter our spirits so
we're unable to love the Lord or others.
What isn't guided or made by God will perish.
Let's fulfill the goal to change. Every
moment offers opportunities
to make that conscious effort to change our thoughts
and all wrong ways. But this is not the work
of a single day; it is the work of a lifetime.
As we study the lives and works of others
who have gone before, let's not be
discouraged; instead we'll follow their examples.
Yes, we'll follow their high aim by loving
God and others, by obeying the word of God,

by asking for and believing in forgiveness
and God's great love for us, even as we learn.
This knowledge is like gold tried in the fire,
or like a precious jewel, and yet it seems
forgotten in the world. Let's learn it well
so we can share it, although we know
that each one must decide for himself.

33 As long as we live, our natures are subject to change.
One moment we are glad, the next we are sad;
now pleased then displeased; devout and then not;
now energetic then lazy; now depressed
then cheerful. The wise will try to stay stable through all
such moods, without acting on the basis of
emotion alone. The winds of change may blow
about, but if our whole intent is to stay
well balanced, to gain in virtue, and keep the intent
directed to God, we'll stand steadfast through all
our troubles. The surer the intent, the more
stable we will remain in every storm.
Yet sometimes the eye of the soul grows clouded when
we behold the delights of the world and the flesh.
To keep the eye bright and clear, we'll choose to rise
above all passing things and keep
our gaze toward God.

34 Let us keep God all in all. What more
could we desire? Let's love God's word more
than we love the world. We'll study the word
and work to understand its meaning, taking
our pleasure in those studies. When we read
or hear the word, we feel God's presence in it.

God makes the heart feel restful and brings us joy.
Then we understand the truth; then
we'll use good judgment in making our decisions.
Praise the Lord! Without this consciousness,
nothing works as well. Through God's grace
and the spice of wisdom, we savor everything.
Worldly people who savor delights of the flesh
won't find this kind of lasting joy; their wisdom
often becomes mere vanity. The pleasures
of the senses also cannot last.
Those who follow God, subduing other
desires, grow wise. They're led from vanity
to truth, from sensual pleasures to spirit-growth.
They clearly see the difference between
Creator and the creature, eternity
and time. Without God, worldly wisdom becomes
vain; but those who follow God grow wise.
God's everlasting light surpasses all.
It sends down rays to clarify and gladden
the heart, to quicken the spirit with the power
of that light. When will we see
the blessed hour when God is acknowledged as
our all in all? Without that gift of faith
and firm belief, there's no real joy.
It saddens us that our wills must often battle
the will of God. Rebellion keeps us far
from finding peace. But we'll always be helped
when we turn to God for strength.

35 In this life we're never free from trouble
or temptation. We need strong spiritual
defense—the armor of prayer and the shield

of patience. To those who overcome is promised angel's food! Why seek rest here, in this life, when we shall only find our rest in the life to come? Instead, we can develop patience, do good work, study, and pray. Our rest and our reward will be in heaven. For the love of God we can endure all things. Our labors, sorrows, temptations, vexations, anguish, neediness, sickness, pain, oppression, confusion, corrections and reproof, disdain—all these experiences help us grow. They can make us strong. The Lord gives glory and reward to those who love him through this transitory life.
Even the saints were often tempted. They too felt sorrow and despair but bore it all with patience. They trusted more in God than in themselves, knowing that the present suffering was temporary and could not compare with heaven's everlasting glory. Wait on the Lord. Be brave, and God will make you strong. Trust the Lord and offer both body and soul to him. You'll be supported and led, for God is always with us, to help us in every way.

36 A clear conscience keeps us from worrying about those who judge us. We can place our minds and intent on God. The meek trust God, not self. It is not possible to please everyone; even Paul, who tried

to please the Lord and save the people, was judged
by others. He served as well as he could, yet still
he was despised. So he committed all
to God, who knows all things; then once more
he armed himself with patience for those who were
against him. Why should we dread any mortal,
who today is here and tomorrow is not? If
we love the Lord we need not fear any
man or woman. What can any human
do to another person's soul?
They hurt themselves more than they hurt you;
in the end no one escapes the judgment.
Let's keep the love of God in our hearts.
If, for a time, we suffer with no visible
reason, we shall lift our hearts
to God, who will deliver us.

37 We can choose to be a loving, giving
person and thus find the Lord. Let us
give up following the personal will
to follow God, putting aside our selfish ways.
When we give ourselves to God, our strength
to follow is increased. We can pray:

Always and in every hour
in great things and in small
may I follow you, my Lord,
to give my all—for all.

38 God must find us emptied of our own will,
else how can we be God's and God be ours?

The sooner we can do this and the better
it is done, the more we please our God.
Some may give themselves, but with exceptions
and without full trust. They still trust more
in self as all-sufficient. Others give
themselves to God, but when temptation comes
they turn back to their own wills and to all
their former ways. They may never find
the satisfaction they might have gained through service
to God and others. To find such inner peace
in heart and soul, let us stand stable in God.
We can keep trying to find this freedom of spirit.
We'll pray for it, study for it, and always desire it.
The cares of this world will fade away, and
our immoderate fears and inordinate loves
will die in us as we trust in God.
Christ tells us to be diligent, to practice
self-control and rule ourselves in all
we do; for we are lord and governor
of our own deeds. As children of God, we have
the freedom of choice. We can choose to live
in the present, yet believe in the eternal.
We can regard all transitory things
while contemplating the everlasting good,
and use our possessions for good purposes
without allowing them to rule over us,
or causing us to become out of balance.
In all events we must not judge anything
by outward appearances. We can silently
enter into prayer, requesting guidance;
soon we'll be shown how to perceive the event
and direct our thought, or word or deed with love.

Moses went into God's tabernacle
to resolve his doubts. There he asked
for help, as well as help for all his people.
So should we retreat into the secret
tabernacle of the heart, where we
can always ask for help.

39 Let us commit ourselves, first, to God.
We wish we could gladly commit all things instead
of clinging to this world. Too often, our
affections and desires will drive us from
one vain thing to another. And yet our very
perfection lies in always considering others
as we would want to be considered. This
golden rule, when followed, brings us to God.
But enemies of the soul resist our respect
for others and our love for God. They taunt
and tempt us. Day and night they try to catch us,
unaware, in a trap of lies.
We must watch and pray to recognize
those traps, and not give in to temptation.

40 We ask the Lord: "Who are we that you
are mindful of us? What have we done for you
that allows us your gifts and grace?" We feel so humble.
Yet still we fret and fear, forget God's love,
give in to temptation, and often complain.
Why should we complain, even if
we sometimes feel forsaken? Let us pray!

Lord, you are here! You ever shall be here—
always good, righteous, and holy,

disposing all things wisely.
But I'm more prone to weakness than to strength,
and I don't always turn to you.
May my heart be fixed, not changeable. Amen.

May we always trust in the grace of God,
although we know that we're unworthy.
Why should we glorify ourselves? It's
dangerous to the soul. It takes away
whatever joy we find and robs us of
God's grace. Sometimes, when we seek to please
ourselves, we may displease the Lord. When we
delight in praises of the world, we can
lose sight of God's importance to us. Our
true praise and joy should rest in God, not self;
whatever good we do must be in honor of God's name,
not our own. May God be praised;
let God's work be magnified; be thankful
for God's goodness. To truth and mercy and
the Trinity be glory, honor, praise.

41 Let's not feel envious when we see others
honored while we're considered less, or
not at all. We are here in darkness,
and often we're deceived. We become
confused. But if we raise our hearts to God,
events on earth will little grieve us. We'll
continue to honor, praise, and glorify
the Lord. Until we bring ourselves to this,
we cannot be at peace nor firmly established
in God; we cannot be enlightened nor
fully united with God.

42 If we look for peace in any person,
we shall remain unsure and discontented.
But we can turn to the everlasting truth—
that is, to God. Then any loss will not
completely overwhelm us, and all our dear
ones are referred to God, even more
beloved in God, who makes us one.
Without that love divine, all other loves
cannot endure. Let's keep all worldly affections
in their place. So much as we draw near
to God, we turn less to comforts of
the world. God seeks a simple, cheerful heart
to occupy, with grace in great abundance.
We're created to be happy, yet
without depending too much on others for
our joy. We gain in spiritual growth
when we learn that anything immoderate
or intemperate, any lack
of balance in our lives, can quickly block
the love and devotion we should hold for God.

43 Let us not be quickly moved by clever
words; God's kingdom is not found in word
alone but in the power. Although words can
enlighten us and give us understanding,
bring remorse for wrongs and comfort souls,
we should read to understand yet still
remember the Source of all. Otherwise
our gain is small. With God placed first, we gain
much more; we learn that knowledge should be shared.
Let us read without intent to be
considered clever or even wise; let's crush

our pride and know that learning seldom tells
us how to serve the Lord. God sometimes gives
more understanding to the simple heart,
illumines it to receive true wisdom, and those
to whom God speaks grow wise in spirit.
God speaks without the sound of words; we
are told to seek eternal life, to turn
from worldliness, to bear wrongs patiently,
and place our trust in God. A time will come
when every conscience is examined and
all souls are searched with the light of God. And then
the thoughts and deeds of all are opened, and all
excuses or vain arguments will cease.
God speaks to those who love him: to some he comes
through study, to some through pain,
to others through prayer.
God manifests to some in ordinary
ways—to others, special. To some, God comes
with signs, to others through an understanding of
the written word. In books there is one voice,
one letter that is read, yet it informs
not everyone alike. God is secretly
hidden in the word: Teacher of truth,
searcher of the heart, promoter of
good works, and reward of all.

44 We gain much when we don't try to know
everything there is to know. We
can turn a deaf ear to many things and think
of what will benefit our inner peace,
our soul. We can turn the eye of the soul

away from whatever may displease us. We
can allow others to hold opinions
that seem best to them, rather than
to argue. If we're established in God and believe
God's judgments, we can be content even
as we're judged by others, or even when
we're overcome. We can be as brave
as Christ was in his suffering.
If we're not yet firmly established in God,
we may sometimes wonder what will ever
become of us! We weep so much about
a little loss. With all our might, we seek
for worldly gain yet give but little thought
to gains of soul and spirit. Why do we
not recognize what's most necessary
to the soul? Because we seek and find
our joy in other things—and rest in them,
which in the end endangers the soul. Let
us learn—and remember—to seek God first.

45 We ask the Lord to help us when we find
ourselves in trouble. We may turn to others,
but in vain, for friendships often change.
We all have weaknesses; we are too ready
to deceive or be deceived. How can
we keep from falling into falseness? If
we trust in God and try to follow the truths
taught by our Lord, we won't easily lapse.
And if it happens, we'll be delivered soon.
Who trusts in God is not forsaken; God
is faithful always. Let's affirm our trust:

My mind is established in God.
I'm fully grounded in Christ.
I shall not fear
nor shall I be moved
by other people's words.

Who can either foresee or prevent bad times?
We're merely human, but we believe in God
who warns us to be aware of human frailty.
We pray that we will neither be betrayed
nor ever betray another. It's best to seek
God first then open our hearts fully to
a very few. God knows us all. As much
as possible, we can avoid being drawn
too much into the lives of others. We
can offer help without becoming too
attached; the ultimate choice is theirs, and we
must recognize that human help can only
reach so far. Let's encourage returning
to God. This frail life is full of temptations,
of the greedy and envious who seek material gain.
But this fine life is also full of those
who love and serve as blessings to us all.
Let's bless both kinds, and leave them to God.

46 Words fly through the air, and it may seem
a very small thing to receive such hasty words.
Yet, because we're human, they hurt us and
we wish more than we should to please. We fear
rejection. Let us try to see ourselves,
and the world, just as we are. Too great
a wish to please another can be a fault.

Let us stand firm in our faith, desiring first to please the Lord. Should we be troubled by what God allows? Let's remember that God does not judge by outward appearances.

O God, be our strength and comfort in all necessities.
Forgive us for not being patient.
Give us grace to endure, continuing in love.
By ourselves we are nothing. Amen.

47 The Lord replies to us:

Do not be broken by impatience with
any work you've taken on for my sake.
Don't let your troubles cause despair.
Remember my promises. You'll be rewarded
more abundantly than you can know.
Your labor here is not for long, nor will
it always be so heavy. Take time to pray.
A day will come when troubles cease,
for all things pass with time.
Work faithfully for me;
my world will be your reward.
Write, read, sing, mourn, pray; endure
adversity. My kingdom is worth more
than all these things. Peace will come,
and death will be no more.
That everlasting day holds infinite clarity,
steadfast peace, and eternal rest.

If we could see the glory of God's saints, who often were despised and persecuted,

we would not complain so much about
our present troubles. Let's think more frequently
of heaven and its saints and God.

48 We wish for the day of eternity to dawn,
to bring all temporal things to an end.
This blessed day now shines upon the saints
with everlasting radiance. But
to pilgrims here on earth, it's far away.
Now we see as through a mirror, darkly.
Sometimes we're filled with fear or burdened with
emotions; we busy ourselves with foolishness
or become obsessed with work. Then
we ask, when can we keep our minds on God?
When shall we have peace, within and without,
and how can we be devoted, steadfast, and sure?
Let us not become so blinded by
temptation or overcome with worldly delights
that we forget to turn to God and pray.

Lord, when may we behold you in full glory?
When will you become our all in all?
May we someday dwell
within your kingdom,
as you have told from the beginning.
We feel like strangers and exiles here—
we ask your help and plead for inward peace. Amen.

We want all heavenly things, but the world
and our own passions pull us down. We wish
to rise above them, yet we're subject to
the flesh. So we fight ourselves: Spirit desires

to go up and flesh compels us down.
Inwardly we suffer; our souls want heaven,
but multitudes of carnal thoughts
soon penetrate the mind.

God, stay close.
Send the lightening of your grace and love.
Help us cast away our foolish fantasies.
Help us overcome our vanity and pride;
take away our fear, doubt, and despair;
our jealousy, envy, and regret.
Forgive us when we do not think of you.
We go to where thought leads us—help us remember
to place you first, O Lord, who said, "Where
your treasure is, there will your heart be, too." Amen.

If we love heaven, we'll gladly speak of it,
and of God. If we love the soul,
we'll take delight in all that's beneficial
to soul's health. But if we love the world
too much, we take more joy in its delights
than in developing our spiritual growth.
Blessed are those who learn to live a balanced,
moderate life in this world, keeping God first.

49 Let us open our hearts and be thankful for
the desire to know and love the Lord. It comes,
not of ourselves or our own doings, but
as a gift of grace. God loves us and wants us to gain
strength of spirit. Let's turn to God, love,
and serve with all our hearts. A common proverb
says that a fire may burn but the flame cannot

ascend without some smoke. We're drawn toward spirit
but can't avoid the smoke of carnal loves.
Our motives are often mixed, and we act to our
own advantage. Let's not ask what we
can gain, but what is acceptable to God.
Let's prefer God's will before our own.
God knows of our desires. We wish to gain
the highest good in heaven but it cannot
yet be given. There is a time for work
and a time for proof. We'll gain if we
can be patient, for here on earth we must
be proved. We may receive some comfort, yet not
in fullest measure. For now, take comfort in
the Lord and be as strong in doing as in
enduring all that happens. Often we must do
the things we'd rather not, and forget
the things we'd like to do. What pleases others
will help us grow, but what pleases ourselves will not.
What others may say is heard, but what we say
is not. Others ask and may receive; we
may ask and be denied. Others are praised,
but of us no word is said. For this, by nature
we resent, and yet we win a battle
if we bear such things in secret, without
complaint. There's nothing more important than
overcoming self by learning to be
content when all things go against one's will.
Such labors bring good fruit; the soul is rewarded
with growth. We feel no pain in our work
to develop the soul because the Holy Spirit
sees our own goodwill and gives us comfort.

For the little we give up on here on earth,
we'll find in heaven all that we desire.
There, we shall possess true goodness,
with no fear of loss. Our wills shall be
at one with the will of God. There, we find
no resistance, no complaints, nothing
to hinder or halt us. In heaven, all the powers
of the soul will be fulfilled. The lowest
place on earth can yield seats high in heaven.
Bow meekly now. Do not care too much
what others say or do, but with a loving,
joyful heart just do your best. Let others
seek for this or that, let others be praised;
take joy yourself in fulfilling the will of God.

50 When in despair or feeling desolate,
we can say these words in prayer:

Lord, let me find my joy in You,
not in myself. You are my hope, my joy,
my crown, and all my honor. All things are yours.
My spirit has been heavy and often troubled
with the passions of the world and flesh.
I ask for inward peace. Without
your help, I cannot have it. A time has come
for me to be proved; the hour now comes that you
have known from the beginning.
I feel broken by sickness and suffering.
If I must suffer for a time, I shall
endure it for your sake. Nothing on earth
is done without your providence,

or without a cause. Now I'm afflicted
so I'll learn your laws and put away
my pride and my presumption. When I feel
confused, it's only so I'll learn to seek
your help rather than to seek from others.
I thank you for your love and saving grace.
I'm learning to trust in you, whose discipline
and correction teaches me. Under that rod
I wholly submit. Help me bend my will
to you. It's better to be corrected here
and now than in a time to come.
You know all things; nothing in my conscience
can stay hidden. You know what's best for me, and
how trouble purges error from the soul.
Do with me what you will. Grant me the grace
to discern all things, visible and invisible.
Above all, help me know your will
and follow it. Amen.

51 We can't always be devout. We bear
the weight of our corruptible bodies. We
feel sorry for the discord between body and soul.
It keeps us from being as spiritual as
we want to be. But we can turn ourselves
to good works and to prayer. Patiently
we'll bear this separation from true home
until we're delivered from our restlessness.
When God comes, we shall forget our labors.
Quietness of soul will then be ours.
So let us say, with spiritual joy,

"The sufferings of this present time cannot
compare with the glory to be revealed!"

52 We often feel unworthy to receive
God's love and consolation. Many times
we've faltered, but God is merciful
and showers us with blessings, more than we
deserve. God's consolation is no fable;
it is true. We confess our faults
to gain God's mercy and forgiveness. The Lord
forgives and also forgets our wrongs.
With true contrition and a loving heart,
we find the hope of pardon. A troubled conscience
can be cleared, and the grace that we once lost
can be recovered. A meek and loving heart
is like a precious balm, acceptable
to God. A broken, contrite heart
will find its home in God.

53 Grace is precious. It is pure, unmixed
with any private loves or worldly comforts.
If we'd have this gracious gift, we
must turn away from all that hinders us
from grace. We can choose a secret place
to pray. We can love to be alone,
turn away from foolish talk, and ask
for a good, clean conscience and
a contrite heart. Let's think less of the world.
Let us choose to serve the Lord before
all others. We can withdraw from worldliness
as much as we can. Saint Peter prayed that we

might see ourselves as strangers and pilgrims on
this earth, placing little value on it and
not be ruled by worldly things. If
we truly want to grow in spirit, we
must know ourselves. The perfect victory
is to have conquered self. One who knows
the self lets sense obey reason and, in turn,
lets reason obey the Lord. We overcome
the self to become the lord of our own world.
To come to that point, let us set the ax
to the root of the tree and cut away self-love,
as well as the love of material things. Then
we'll find serenity and peace of conscience.
Yet only a few are willing to die to self.

54 Human nature and grace often move
in opposite ways. Those who have been touched
by grace will understand. Although we all
may desire the good and pretend to it in words
and deeds, we're often deceived by nature, who draws
us to herself. She entraps us; she seeks
out her own gain. But grace walks simply, declining
all wrong and pretending to nothing. Grace acts purely
for God, in whom she rests. Human nature
dies hard. She'll neither be oppressed
nor overcome, nor easily subjected.
Grace resists the senses and
is easily overpowered. Grace loves
a holy discipline; she desires
to live for God. She doesn't wish to rule.
For God, she bows to creatures. She asks not what

may profit herself, but what will profit the many.
Nature works to her own advantage. While nature
enjoys all honor and praise, grace refers
all reverence to God. Nature resents
rebukes, but grace receives them as gifts of God.
Nature loves to be idle. Grace cannot
be idle without doing some good deed.
She seeks out useful work. Nature desires
everything pleasant, fair, and new; she
despises all that's common, low, and old.
Grace delights in simplicity; she won't
refuse to wear old clothes or simple styles.
Human nature loves all worldly things
and seeks out worldly gain. With any loss,
she sorrows. She's quickly moved by clever words.
But grace beholds the everlasting truth.
She doesn't trust the world; she is not troubled
at things lost, for her treasure lies
in God and the spiritual things that never perish.
But human nature covets worldly goods.
She more gladly takes than gives; she loves
possessions. Grace takes pity on the poor.
She's generous, avoiding personal profit.
She's content with little and knows it is
more blessed to give than to receive.
Nature loves creatures and the flesh. She runs
about to see new things. But grace will draw
us to the love of God and to the love
of virtue. She renounces inordinate loves,
subdues desire, and uses restraint.
As much as possible, she keeps to herself.

Human nature seeks much outward comfort,
but grace seeks comfort in God and delights in the good.
Nature seeks her own benefit and gain,
hoping always for profit, praise, and fame;
she expects her every deed to be
considered great. But grace seeks nothing in
this world and no rewards but God. She
uses worldly goods only enough
to gain the everlasting good. She
cares nothing for the praises of the world.
Nature takes much joy in friends and kin;
she's proud of her education or noble blood.
She likes to be with people she considers
to be important; she flatters the rich and prefers
those whom she feels are superior, or
as noble as she. But grace will love her enemy
and takes no pride in worldly friends. To her,
virtue ranks higher. She favors the poor. She joys
in truth. She helps others to grow in goodness, and
daily she seeks for higher gifts of grace.
She wishes all of us to follow Christ.
Nature often complains, but grace bears all
in quietness. Nature is selfish, striving
and fighting for herself, but grace consigns
everything to God. She ascribes
no goodness to herself, submitting to
the eternal wisdom and judgment of the Lord.
Nature loves a secret, to hear about
things new. She craves experience and wishes
to be known, to do great things for which
she will be praised. But grace cares not about

the new or curious; she knows that from
such vanities may come corruption;
that nothing new may long endure upon
the earth. Grace teaches us restraint.
In any quest for knowledge, art, or science
she seeks out spiritual gain, with all her praise
and honor given to the Lord. She hopes
only to be blessed in all her works.
Grace is a supernatural light, a gift
of God, the mark of the elect.
It takes us from the love of earth up to
the love of heaven. The more nature is overcome,
the more the gift of grace is given.
Through grace the soul is re-formed,
more and more to the image of God.

55

O Lord, who made me to your image and
to your likeness, grant me grace.
You've shown me I must overcome
my human nature, which draws me toward wrong.
I can't resist my selfish, sensual nature
without your grace. I have great need of it. Amen.

Since Adam fell, our natures' innate good
has been corrupted, so now we're drawn to wrong.
The innate good in nature is like a spark
dimmed by ashes. Thus our natural reason,
although dimmed by ignorance, can judge
between the good and evil, true and false.
Our human nature won't let us do what we
approve. We do not clearly see the light.

In the reason of my soul
I delight in the law and in
Your teachings, knowing they are good
and righteous and holy. I know what's wrong
and what must be avoided. Yet still I obey my sensuality
rather than my reason. So it follows that I will
to be good but fail to follow. My purpose is
to do good deeds, but for lack of grace I fail.
I know the way to go but I'm burdened with
this body and am slow to come to You.
How necessary is your grace for me
to begin well, to continue, and to end well.
Without You I do nothing good.
O heavenly grace, come to me and help! Amen.

Without God neither work nor wealth, beauty
or strength, wit or eloquence matters. The gifts of nature
are common to both good and bad, but grace
and love are gifts that show us worthy of heaven.
This grace is so valued that neither the gift
of prophecy nor the gift of knowledge can be
without her. Even faith and hope and other
virtues are not acceptable to God
without the grace of charity.
This blessed grace can make the poor in spirit
rich in virtue. It makes one who is rich
in worldly goods be meek in heart.

Come into my soul, O Lord.
Fill me with your spiritual comfort.
Let me not fail or faint, be weary or dry

of spirit. May I find grace in your sight;
for grace is sufficient even when I want
the things my nature desires.
With grace, I need not fear temptation or trouble.
Grace is my strength, my comfort, my counsel, and
my help. She is stronger than my enemies,
wiser than all the world. Grace is mistress
of truth, teacher of discipline, the light of the heart,
the comfort of trouble. Grace guards me from fear
and drives away my sorrow. She nourishes
devotion and brings tears to the devout.
All these things are grace. What am I
without her?—a dry stick to be thrown away.
Grant that grace will follow me, to make
me ever busy in good works till death. Amen.

56 As we get out of ourselves, we may enter into God. By the forsaking of self we join ourselves unto our Lord. Let us follow Christ and resign ourselves into God's hands, remembering the words:

Follow me, for I am the Way,
the Truth, and the Life.

Without a way no one can go,
without the truth no one can know,
without the life no one can live.
Christ is the way to go, the truth to believe,
and the life for which we hope. The way can't be

defiled; the truth can't be deceived; the life
shall have no end. Christ is the way most straight,
the truth most perfect, the life most sweet—
a blessed life. If we abide in the way,
we'll know the truth that delivers us
to everlasting life. Christ declared:

If you want that life, keep my commandments.
If you'd know the truth, believe my teachings.
If you would be perfect, help the poor.
If you'd be my disciple, forsake yourself.
If you'd have the blessed life, despise this present one.
If you'd be high in heaven, be meek on earth.
If you'd rule with me, bear the cross with me,
for only servants of the cross shall find the blessed, everlasting life.

The Lord's way is narrow, despised in this world.
We ask for grace to bear the world's scorn.
No servant is greater than his lord,
and no disciple is above his master.
May these servants learn the way, for in it
is our health and our perfection.
Whatever we read or hear otherwise
neither refreshes nor delights us. As much
as we've read all these words and know them well,
we'll be blessed if we can fulfill them. Christ said:

Those who keep my commandments are those
who love me. And those who love me are loved by God,
and I will love them and show myself to them,
and let them sit with me in my Father's kingdom.

A PRAYER

O Lord, as you have promised, let it be done.
We'll bear the cross of repentance; it leads to you.
We go forth together for your sake.
We'll take up our burdens for you;
for you we persevere.
You are our help, our leader, and our guide. Amen.

57 Patience in adversity will please
the Lord more than devotion in prosperity.
Why should a little trouble make us sad?
It will pass. As long as we may live,
it's not the first nor shall it be the last.
We can be brave when we're not troubled; we
give counsel and strengthen others with our words.
But when adversity knocks at our door,
our strength may fail because we are so frail.
Let's strengthen ourselves to do the best we can.
When troubles come we may be sad yet not
be overwhelmed. We can suffer in patience
and wait for better times. When we feel low
let's not lash out or hurt another. Soon
our sorrow will be eased and once again
life will be sweet. The Lord is near to help
and comfort, when we ask. Let's be quiet
of heart and prepare ourselves for sorrow.
Although we often feel troubled and tempted,
all is not lost. We're only human, not angels.
God comforts the suffering and lifts up all

who acknowledge their faults, so they are established in God.
The words of the Lord are wholesome, sweeter than honey
to our mouths. Whatever troubles we
may suffer for God, we'll come at last
to everlasting health. May we have
a good end to this life, a blessed passage
and a straight way into the kingdom of God.

58 We should not question the ways of God:
Why one seems forsaken and another in grace;
why one is troubled while another seems to advance.
All these things surpass our knowledge. When
we ask, "Why?" we should recall David's reply:

The Lord is righteous.
True and upright are the judgments of God,
and not to be feared or questioned,
for we cannot comprehend.

Let's not waste ourselves in argument
or doubt. The Lord is not a god of strife
but of peace and love. Before the world
was made, God knew the beloved ones.
God knows the first one and the last
and loves us all with unchanging, invaluable love.
Those who despise the least of God's children
does no honor to the greatest. For we
are One, united and knit together in one
sure bond of perfect love. Those beloved
of God love the Lord much more than themselves.
Nothing can turn them from God's love. They

are filled with eternal truth; they burn with a love
that cannot be quenched. But those who remain
worldly and selfish do not consider God's saints.
They have no spiritual understanding. Although
they have natural affections, their loves are not
of the spirit. They merely imagine heavenly things.
Those illumined with grace behold the spiritual.
Let's hope to be worthy with the least of God's holy ones.
We're most acceptable to God when we
consider how little is our virtue and
how great are all our faults. It's better to pray
that we may be more holy and grow in love.
It would be great to be the least in heaven,
where all are great. We are God's children. Christ said:

Unless you become as little children,
you cannot enter into heaven.

Whoever humbles self, like a child,
can enter in the kingdom. Never disdain
to be as meek as a child. The proud and the rich
will have their comforts here, but a good, poor person
may enter while they weep outside the gate.
Be happy to be meek and gentle;
yours will be the kingdom. Walk on your way in truth.

59 Who can we trust in this life? Where
can be our solace and comfort under heaven?
Is it not the Lord, whose mercy is not
measured? When has anything
gone well without God—or when has it

gone poorly with God? We'd rather be poor with God
than rich without. We'd rather be like pilgrims
in this world. Where God is, there
is heaven. Where God is not, there is both death
and hell. God is all we desire.
We pray for help in our necessities;
God is our hope, our trust, our comfort, and
our faithful help in every need. We
must seek whatever we may need, but God
seeks only our spiritual gain.
God turns all things to the best. We're given temptations
and troubles to prove ourselves; for this proof
let's be thankful and praise the Lord as much
as when we are in comfort. Let us put
our trust in God and patiently bear our troubles.
We shall learn that all we do without
the Lord is folly. Unless God comforts, counsels,
assists, informs, and defends us, there is no help.
Counselors don't always give wise counsel; nor
can doctors' knowledge always bring us health.
Riches don't deliver us. All
that's meant to help is worth nothing if God
is absent—for God is the end and beginning of all
good things. To trust in God is comfort. We lift
ourselves to God, trusting that our souls
will be blessed. May nothing within us
offend the eye of God.

Lord, hear our prayers—
defend us from dangers in this life,
and through your grace direct our ways. Amen.

Book Four

On Understanding Why Communion Is Important

1 We find it hard to believe the words of Christ—

Come unto me, all who labor and
are heavy-laden, and I will give you rest.

Yet how sweet those words can sound when we take communion. We wonder how can we presume to come? Yet even when we cannot comprehend, our Lord repeats, *"Come to me!"* Before receiving communion we can pray:

Lord, your words we thankfully accept.
These are words you've spoken: now they're ours
and we receive them gladly.
They're planted in our hearts—these words of love.

When we recall our faults we feel afraid
to face this mystery, and then we may
withdraw. We think of how we want to please you
yet know how little we do—
how few hours of our busy lives we take
to live for your sake. Our minds are set
too much upon the world. Help us prepare
ourselves to be worthy of your love,
to believe we are a part of you,
and through you will receive eternal life. Amen.

We travel far to marvel at some sight
or worldly wonder but find it all is vain.
Let's remind ourselves that God is here,
within us, at the altar of the heart.
If communion would be fruitful, we
must come with faith, devotion, hope, and love.

O God, maker of all of us,
we marvel at everything you do.
How graciously you bring your love to us
in this holy sacrament.

Within communion lies a hidden grace.
Virtues of the soul, once lost, can be
restored, and beauty, dimmed by faults, returned.
Our minds and bodies can recover strength.
Yet we stay slow and negligent to go;
we don't allow ourselves to love the Lord,
in whom we'd find redemption and hope. Here in
this world God offers comfort, and
to all in heaven, eternal rest. Yet

we still ignore communion. In the hardness
of our hearts we reject this gift. If
communion were given in only one place
and consecrated by only one leader in
the world, wouldn't everyone go running
to that place or to that person, just
to witness the mystery that gladdens heaven and
preserves the world? Now Christ is offered to many.
The more this sacrament is spread, the more
God's grace and love is shown.
Let's be thankful that we
can be so easily refreshed.

2 We come to God, trusting in goodness and mercy,
as an invalid turns to a healer or as one
who thirsts will come to the fountain of life.
We come in desolation to seek for comfort.
But how does the Lord come to us? And who are we
to be given so much? Dare we appear before
our Maker? We often feel unworthy, yet
we must remind ourselves that God's creations
are all made perfect—and so praise God! Let
us offer thanks, always. Even when
we don't deserve it, God's feast of forgiveness
and love divine is ours.

O God, how marvelous is your work,
how mighty your virtue and goodness,
how true your truth!
By your word all things are made.
It's far above our understanding
that you are Lord of all,

that you need nothing from us.
By this sacrament you dwell in us.
Help us keep our hearts attuned to you
so we may come, with good conscience,
to celebrate your love.
May our souls be glad
for the gift of communion. Amen.

As we take this sacrament,
God works with us to redeem our souls. When
we take communion, we partake of the
boundless grace and love of Jesus.
Christ's mercy is never diminished. So with
communion, both body and mind are renewed. We
feel joyful, as if it were the day that Christ
was born—or as if, on this day,
he died for us.

3 Through that joy we come to Christ again.
In God is all that we desire: our health,
redemption, hope, and strength—our honor and glory.
The soul lifts up to receive the Lord with love,
reverence, and awe. We desire
to be one with God, and love is sufficient for
that sacred union. We know there is no comfort
without the Lord; without our Maker we
cannot be, and without God's presence
in our lives we never truly live.
We receive communion for our health.
It strengthens us. When we sincerely partake
of this sacrament, we are blessed.
So often we're reluctant, but let us now

renew ourselves with prayer, confess our faults,
and rekindle a fervor of spirit so we
will not forget our purpose. From our youth
we're proud and inclined to wrong, but the love
of God can keep us from falling, worse and worse.
Communion draws us away from wrong thinking and
inclines us more toward goodness. Although we may
not receive the sacrament each day, we can
partake at times convenient. As long as we
are in this mortal body, let's remember
our Lord through communion.

Lord, we're thankful that you come to us.
You refresh the needs of the soul;
you fill us with spiritual joy!
You alone—above all things—we love.
Let all be still in your presence. Amen.

4 May we be worthy of this gift of love.
May our hearts be moved toward God as we
overcome our idleness and pray
that we'll receive the grace to know
within our soul the hidden sweetness
of this blessed sacrament. It is
a fountain of abundance! May we behold
the mystery; may our belief be strengthened.
For it is God's—not given by our power
or invention. No one understands
such mysteries; no one is sufficient of
one's self. With a simple heart, and
in faith, we come. We believe

that God is here. We ask for mercy and
for special grace that we may melt and flow
in our Lord's love. Communion is the life
of soul and body, remedy of spiritual
illness, the means by which a vice is cured,
a passion controlled, temptation overcome.
Through holy communion hope is strengthened and
faith is firmly established. Charity
and love are kindled here. Those in deep
despair are given hope, and lives renewed.
When we feel cold and dull, grace enlightens
us to make us fervent followers
of Christ, with spirits quickening!
Who comes to the fountain without finding relief?
Who stands by a fire without feeling its heat?
God is the fountain of sweetness, the fire that burns
forever and never fails. Even when
we may not draw the fountain's fullness, we
can put our mouths to it and take some sweet drops
so we're not dried away. We may not be
as full of charity as angels, yet
through communion we can prepare our hearts
for God. Whatever we may lack, we'll ask
God to supply. Daily we work in the sweat
of our bodies, heart-weary with sorrow, and often we
are troubled by temptation. No one can help
or deliver us or make us safe but God.

Lord, I commit myself
and all that's mine to you,
to lead me to eternal life.
Accept me, Lord.

Increase my love and my devotion
through communion. Amen.

5 If we were pure as angels and holy as saints
we might be worthy to receive communion.
But we're not, and yet it's offered to us—
this mystery of God's boundless love.
Great are responsibilities of those
who offer it—these ministers of God
who repeat Christ's words of consecration.
We're all subject to God's will and we
believe in God, above the self. We come
with awe and reverence; and after, we
must keep an even stronger discipline.

6 What can we do to be more worthy of
God's love? We can ask to be shown the way:

Lord, teach us day by day and hour by hour
how to prepare for holy communion with you.
Create in us a loving heart. Amen.

7 We shall celebrate this sacrament
with reverence, with faith, and humble intent.
Daily we'll examine our conscience, and through
our prayers and true remorse we'll make it clean,
so nothing can stop us from freely taking part
in holy communion. May all our faults displease us.
May we feel sorry for our faults, and for
any offenses we have given. In
our secret heart we shall confess our faults,

for we neglect the spiritual; slow
to sympathize and hard of heart are we.
We're open to ease and closed to repentance; we rush
to hear and see what's new, and we're impatient
with those who are old or ill. We seek to gain,
yet we're slow to give. We're quick to speak,
and reluctant to be silent. We're greedy to feed
the body but not the soul. We're deaf to God's word,
which feeds the soul. We are quick to rest,
yet slow to work; attentive to fables, but not
to holy words. We hurry to reach the end
without considering the way or the means to the end.
Quickly moved to anger and quick to judge
are we; we welcome prosperity but in
adversity we loudly complain. We plan
to do good but seldom follow through. When
we confess we're sorry for our faults
we find renewal of our purpose. Let's
amend our faults and do better. With the full
resigning of the will, we offer ourselves
to the honor of God. Faithfully we can
commit ourselves, body and soul, to
receive communion. There's no greater relief
than to overcome a fault, and wholly
give one's self to God. With this true
repentance we receive forgiveness and
God's grace. Our faults no longer are
remembered, for all is forgiven.

8 Each day we'll offer ourselves to God, just
as Christ gave himself for us. He gave his body
and his blood that we might be his, and he

might be ours. If we were to trust
only in ourselves and not offer
freely, there'd be no perfect union.
This free offering must come before
anything we do, if we're to receive
true liberty and grace. Those who can't
or won't forsake the self are not illumined,
nor are they free. The words of Christ hold true:

Who will not bear his cross and follow me
cannot be my disciple. Come to me with love.

9

A PRAYER

Lord, all in heaven and earth are yours.
I offer myself to you; may I be
with you as you are with me, always.
With a simple heart I offer myself
to your service. Accept me, Lord.
I ask you to put away my offenses,
cleanse my conscience, and restore to me
the grace I've lost. Forgive me for things past.
Receive me into your peace.
All my wrongs displease me; I'm sorry for my mistakes;
I shall not commit them again.
I also offer to you my good deeds, imperfect
as they may be. Help me do better
and bring me to a blessed end. Amen.

We offer prayers for all who request our prayers.
We pray that they may know your grace and love,

your protection from peril and from pain.
May their gratitude lead them to give thanks
and all praise to God. We also pray
for those who give us sorrow, hurt, or grief;
for those we've troubled with our words, thoughts, deeds—
whether we knew it or not. May we be
forgiven for any offense to God or to
each other. May anger be taken from our hearts—
and any hindrance to brotherly love.
We pray for mercy on all who ask for mercy.
We pray for grace to all who need it. May
we all receive God's grace and love, and be
worthy to live at last in eternity.

10 May we come often to communion, to
this fountain of mercy, grace, and goodness. Here
we can be healed of passions and vices, and
made strong to resist temptation. But even
the faithful are sometimes tempted to stay away.
As written in Job, a negative spirit can come
among God's children, to confuse or frighten them
—or to diminish their faith. We despise
that spirit of deceit; we reject
all fantasies and lies! We shall continue
to take communion. We're advised to put
away all doubt, which stops the flow of grace
and destroys our devotion to God. We shall believe;
we can forgive! And if we have offended,
we'll ask forgiveness. We know that God forgives.
Let us not delay, today—for tomorrow
may come with even greater problems. Let
us overcome our lethargy today,

for tomorrow we'll be even lazier!
Not much devotion is seen in those who ignore
communion, but happy are they who partake of it
for when we ask the Lord to quicken us,
our spiritual strength grows even more.
Every day and every hour we
can hold communion of spirit with the Lord.
How? By remembering his suffering
and recalling the wonder of his sacrifice.
When we offer ourselves to God, we're blessed.
We can do this in a common way,
with neither too much nor too little talk.
The way of moderation is always best.

11 Sometimes, during communion, we may weep
for joy! The heart longs for God, who's hidden in
this sacrament. We await the perfect
day when sacraments shall cease, when we
no longer need them. But while we're in this life
we'll be patient; we shall live with faith
and patience. What the saints believed, we can
believe; and for all they hoped we too
can hope. As they came to God by grace,
we trust to come. Meanwhile we'll live by faith,
following those examples. Let's read to be
uplifted, from books that are like a spiritual glass
for us to gaze in. Much is necessary
in this world; but let's remember that
God gives himself to refresh our souls.
God's word is set as a lamp for our feet and a light
for the soul. At communion, two tables are set:
One holds the bread and the wine; the other holds

the Word of God, to instruct us well. Let us
be thankful for that bright, eternal light
and for this supper, prepared with God's great love.
How honorable is the service of those who minister;
how clean should be their hands, how pure their mouths,
how holy their bodies, and undefiled their hearts.
Their speech should be honest, to benefit each soul.
These ministers must pray for grace and love,
for good conscience, and a willing heart
to serve the Lord.

12 God loves goodness and seeks out loving hearts
to dwell within. Let's prepare our hearts
to be a chamber where we keep our Easter.
If we'd have God there, we'll keep it clear
of worldly clamor. We can be solitary
as a sparrow on the roof as we consider
any offenses. Then we'll rid ourselves
of them, knowing God forgives.
Let's prepare the best we can to
receive our Lord, recognizing we
are not sufficient of ourselves. Only
through God's mercy, love, and grace can we
come to communion as we should. We take
this sacrament, not because of custom,
but in awe and reverence, and
with all our love. God has invited us
and will supply our every need. When we
receive this gift, let's thank the Lord. Even
if we feel insincere and dry
of spirit, let's continue to pray for the gift
of devotion. We have need of God,

not God of us. We come here not to sanctify
the Lord but to be sanctified, to be
united with God, so spirits are
rekindled and we are improved. After
we receive the sacrament, let's keep
that spirit of love. Good keeping will prepare
us to receive even more grace from God.
Let us be still, be solitary, and
keep God always in our hearts.
The world can never take this love away.
When we give our all to God, then we'll
be living not for self, but only for God.

13 Through communion we can savor a taste
of things eternal. In that moment, we melt
into God's love and forget ourselves. We are
in God, and God is in us; and we are one.
We love the Lord of peace and rest,
the God who guides a simple heart.
How good is this spirit that refreshes us!
To those who love God all daily needs are given.
What love without measure we are shown;
what can we give back for all this love?
The best thing we can do is give
our hearts to God.

14 How great is the goodness of God! When we think
of the many people over the ages who've come
to communion fervently, we feel shame
to be so cold and apathetic. We wonder
why we take so much for granted and
remain so dry before the fountain of love.

Lord, help us feel your love.
Help our faith recover,
our hope become more perfect, and
our love and charity to be rekindled.
Help us never to fail you. Although
we may not seem as fervent and devout
as others, we still desire the grace to be
numbered among their company. Amen.

15 Let us pray continually to receive
and keep the grace of devotion. Let's
commit ourselves to God. Even when
our love and devotion seem small, we must not feel
discouraged, for God will answer our prayers. With hope
and patience we await; sometimes a fault
can hold us back. Whether our fault is little
or large, we must work to overcome it.
As we give ourselves to God, replacing
our own will with the will of God,
we'll find that union and an inner peace.
So with a simple heart, filled with love,
let us lift our intent to God. We'll turn
away from excessive love of worldly things
in order to receive God's grace, and to
be worthy of the gift of pure devotion.
As we lift our hearts, the grace of God
will come. And when we place ourselves in
the hands of God, cherishing God's love
and honor, we shall be blessed.

16

A PRAYER

Lord, you know my faults and all my needs.
You know how often I am tempted
and troubled. You alone can help.
You know what I need.
I stand before you asking for your grace.
Refresh me with your spiritual food,
rekindle my heart with your love,
enlighten me with understanding. Amen.

17 Although we're not as worthy as God's saints,
we want to receive the Lord. We offer all
the love that's in our hearts. We offer freely
praise and reverence and gratitude. We come
with the hope and faith shown by
the mother of Christ at the time she said:
"Behold the handmaid of the Lord;
be it done to me according to Thy word,"
and as John the Baptist said:
"I present myself to God with all my heart."

18 We should beware of being too curious
about communion, a mystery profound.
We must not drown it in the depths of doubt.
The power of God works more than we can know,
more than we can understand. Blessed
is the simple, trusting heart, untroubled
by idle questioning. Those who choose
the plain and steadfast path of God's commandments

have chosen well. Many lose devotion
in the search for more than they can know.
Faith and trust and honesty, good work
and goodwill are all that's asked of us.
Some may be tempted to doubt their faith,
as well as the purpose of communion;
let's not even try to answer such doubts
but only believe and trust in the Lord.
Let's go on with reverence, humility, and
our faith in the sacrament of communion. What
we can't understand we can commit to God,
who never deceives. All who trust in self
too much are often deceived. Let us love
simplicity and goodness. May we grow
in spirit, be given understanding, and find
much wisdom. Our reason may be feeble but
our faith is stable and true. Reason follows
faith. In this holy sacrament,
love and faith come first. In secret ways
they work above all reason. And God
does great things, both in heaven and on earth.